A DARK STRANGER'S GUIDE TO POLITICS

By Kerron Cross

Synopsis

A humorous book looking at the subject of British politics – from life in Parliament, to life in local government, to getting elected/selected yourself – from the viewpoint of someone who has worked at every level in the political process and has lived to tell the tale!

Chapters:

Introduction – A short introduction explaining why I decided to write the book and what (hopefully) qualifies me to do so. (Page 5)

Chapter 1 – Politics – Setting The Scene Before you explore the world of politics, you have to understand what you mean by 'politics'. Perspective is key. (Page 13)

Chapter 2 – Working in Parliament. An insight into what it's really like to work inside the 'Westminster Bubble'. (Page 34)

Chapter 3 – Enjoying Yourself In Parliament. Over 7,000 people work within the Parliamentary Estate – but working under such immense pressure, how do they relax? (Page 59)

Chapter 4 – Local Government. What's it like to be a local authority representative in the glamorous world of local politics? Find out here. (Page 85)

Chapter 5 – Running For Parliament – Getting Selected. Before you run for public office, you first have to get selected. Here is an insider's guide to the selection process. (Page 103)

Chapter 6 – Running For Parliament – The General Election. Once you do get selected to fight a constituency at the General Election, the next part is the election itself. Are you in a safe seat, a marginal or a completely unwinnable? Whatever you do, don't embarrass yourself! (Page 133)

Chapter 7 – Post Election. Following an election there will be many things a politician wants to do – mainly sleep. Here is a guide to what happens after a General Election. (Page 160)

Chapter 8 – Political Blogging. Giving your unique viewpoint in a unique way. How I became an award winner. (Page 174)

Chapter 9 – Influencing the Political Process. What's the point in voting? Should you get involved yourself? (Page 191)

About the Author – A short biography (Page 208)

Introduction – A Dark Stranger's Guide To Politics.

When looking for a title for this book, I kicked around a few ideas in my head.

Sometimes my head needs a little kicking around – metaphorically, rather than literally. (I have absolutely no interest of turning up to a BNP rally and trying to explain why I find their politics repugnant, as I suspect that I wouldn't get a particularly considered response – though I may well get a boot to the head.)

I started with the working title of *"A Blogger's Guide to Politics"*, then realised that there are several thousand bloggers talking about politics – most of them doing so because: 1) They think they have something unique to say into the political process, and the power of blogging gives them the opportunity to put their undiluted, unspun views into the public square freely 2) No-one will pay for them to put their views into a newspaper, magazine or book format.

I wanted to distinguish what might make my viewpoint different, rather than have an interminable debate about the importance of social media to political discourse. (Yes, it is important, but equally I don't think that most MPs I am *'friends'* with on Facebook have a clue who I am – or, more to the point, care. When one of them attempts to *'poke'* me, I am always tempted to write a headline along the lines of *"MP tries to poke political blogger!"* – then I realise that fighting law suits is both annoying and expensive. Also I do not own a newspaper, so it would be hard for me to write that headline anyway. In all honesty, I've not thought it through in any great depth.)

The other main reason I have steered away from such a title is that I stopped blogging in 2009. For those of you who were fortunate/unfortunate enough to read my blog for the 4 years it ran (the website analytics indicate over 387,263 of you did visit – this suggests to me: 1) the analytics are wrong, 2) the counter on my blog broke a long time ago, 3) both of these things) you will probably spot that the stories, anecdotes and themes in this book are broadly taken from that blog. However it is not a wholesale reproduction, it just takes its inspiration from those pages.

In other words, I nicked lots of my existing material and wanted to pass it off to a new audience with a fresh coat of gloss – and a new set of royalties.

That (bizarrely successful) blog was called *"The Voice of the Delectable Left",* so why not go down that street? In short, I didn't want to go down the route of restricting the readership to those on the Left of politics, or suggest that engaging with politics is something that only people from that section of society should go into.

Politics is for everyone. Whilst political elites and pressure groups of every viewpoint and persuasion try to occupy and control the middle ground, and stop others breaking into it, the reason we have elections and political parties is to ensure everyone has the opportunity to have their say. The process doesn't always work, in fact quite often it doesn't, but I don't want to put anyone off having a go at changing the world for the better – even if they are wrong.

Whether you are Lib Dem, Tory, Labour or anything in between, please do buy this book and do be inspired. I hope that these reflections will make you think that anyone can make a difference if they try hard enough. I may disagree with what you say but I support your right to say it.

Einstein once said: *"Two things are infinite: the universe and human stupidity – and I'm not sure about the universe."* Don't let my inherent daftness put you off changing the world (as if it would!), but do let it show that anyone can make it at least a little way along the political path.

Now if you are a BNP supporter, firstly congratulations on buying this book and having someone read it to you, but I have a short disclaimer to add. I am sorry that this really isn't the book for you, so you may as well put it back on the shelf. Better still, buy the book and be really annoyed about it.

I am afraid that because I believe in values such as fairness and equality – anyone espousing racist, fascist or xenophobic views loses the right to have their say or be taken seriously in the mainstream.

Love thy neighbour. Love thy enemy. Always consider the Common Good. Regardless of your colour, country of birth, sexuality, gender etc etc etc, all are welcome.

So whilst this book is hopefully still delectable, if you come from a different background to me and have a different viewpoint, still come hither, just take my socialist leanings with a teaspoon/ladle full of salt.

Yes, I really did just say *'come hither'*. I won't do it again, I promise.

The other suggestion was *"A Christian Guide to Politics"*. Writing as a Christian – and twisting the arms of Christian publishers who I have the pleasure, honour and sheer coincidence of knowing – that seemed to make a lot of sense. However, as expressed above, I didn't want to exclude anyone. Also describing yourself as a Christian guide to anything is a bit of a minefield.

One of the big misconceptions about people of faith is that they want to tell you how to live your life and take great pleasure in pointing out to you how you are getting things wrong. Actually, I am sure some Christians do that, but I am reminded of the bit in the Bible that says you should take the plank out of your own eye, before you point out the speck of dust in someone else's. Also the overall message of the Bible, unless I've got it horribly wrong (and let's face it, there is every chance I have) is to love everyone, but particularly the poor, the marginalised, the vulnerable, the unloved, the dispossessed and, last but not least, sinners.

For avoidance of doubt, when I say *'sinners'* here I mean *'everyone'*. Me, you, Auntie Jean and the Bonzo Dog Doodah Band. All fall short of perfection and do stuff wrong, the difference with born again Christians is that they hopefully recognise that they are flawed, have messed up in the past and will mess up again in the future. It's about forgiveness rather than retribution. Being a Christian is not about being a *'good person',* it is about grace – being loved even when you don't deserve it.

Having said that, the Bonzo Dog Doodah Band did do some great albums.

So, yes, my politics is informed by my faith – as is the way I live my life. But this doesn't mean I don't get things wrong or that I think I am somehow better than everyone else – in fact I know this not to be the case. It means through humility and service we can hopefully do our little bit to improve the world we live in. I still swear, make toilet jokes and am perpetually bitter about things when I write. I hope you will forgive me for that, but it is who God made me as a person, and to pretend I am someone other than the failed but extremely good looking person I am, would be insincere.

So what does that leave us with for a title? In the end I settled on *"A Dark Stranger's Guide To Politics"*.

The reason was threefold: 1) It's my name – *'Kerron'* comes from the Manx dialect and means *'Dark Stranger'*. (Actually, Wikipedia says different, but I take my Mum's word over that of the internet, any day of the week.) 2) I have just written and published a separate book about the Isle of Man called *"A Dark Stranger's Guide to the Isle of Man"* (please go and buy it, it really is brilliant and hilarious, honest!) and who knows what potential there is here for a revenue-busting best-selling series of books with merchandising spin-offs from such a genius concept. Order your Dark Stranger T-shirts and mugs now. Limited edition. All proceeds go to a good cause…well, me. 3) It might annoy the BNP a bit, because they already think I am foreign anyway.

The only downside with this title, as my wife helpfully pointed out, is that *"A Dark Stranger's Guide"* to anything sounds like I'm writing on behalf of a hard-core dating website. This is a risk I am willing to take – and who knows it may even push up sales – just don't tell my wife that I ignored her advice.

There are two things you should never do. One is argue with your wife. The second is argue with a Glaswegian. Of course if (as in my case) your wife is Glaswegian, you are doubly stuffed on this front. Don't worry though, I have life insurance.*

Thanks for buying the book. I hope you enjoy it.

(*Since writing and publishing this book, my wife has left me and we are going through a divorce. I have spent the intervening months setting up a hard-core dating website.)

1. Politics – Setting The Scene

When writing a book about politics, it's difficult to know where to start. *'Politics'* is one of the most misunderstood words in our lexicon.

Actually, *'lexicon'* would be one of our most misunderstood words if more people had heard of it, but let's not go down that road right now.

If you ask people what they think of when you say *'politics'*, you'd get a mixed reaction - but I'd wager that most people would say things like: *'boring'*, *'liars'*, *'expense cheats'*, *'all the same'*.

Various studies have shown that the majority of the general public believe MPs are all out for themselves, cooking the books and behaving outside of the public interest. The only exception to this rough rule of thumb is when you ask people about their own MP - on the whole, people will then say that this specific individual is a good person, hard-working and doing their bit for the improvement of the local area.

There can be several reasons for this, but I offer just two initial reflections. 1) The vast majority of coverage politicians get in the press is negative. As a corporate entity, they are as popular as estate agents, traffic wardens or tax inspectors. In fact, I know one MP who would tell people when he was *'off duty'* (for example, on holiday; getting his hair cut; or in the back of a breakdown truck with the man from the AA) that he was a tax inspector, just because it was less awkward and meant he generally received less hostility. 2) When people come into contact with their local MP they tend to realise that the person in front of them is a genuine human being who, for the most part, is trying to do their best in a difficult situation.

Whilst the whole idea of the election process can seem a bit outdated with the advent of instant phone and electronic voting for most TV gameshows and reality concepts, when people feel they have a personal interest or investment into a specific election result or candidate, then they can become quite highly motivated. The problem for those wishing to be MPs, there is no way they can strike up a personal relationship or conversation with every one of their constituents. If the average electorate for a parliamentary seat is around 70,000 to 125,000 people, it is impossible to get round everyone in a 5 year electoral cycle, no matter how much you want to or how hard you work. This means, inevitably, that many people have no idea who their local representative is and they automatically believe the doom-mongers whose job it is to shift newspapers on a daily basis.

But *'politics'* is not simply about politicians – and how they work, or don't work, for our best interests. Politics is about the issues that surround our daily lives. Next time someone says they don't do politics ask them what they think about waiting times at their local A&E department, or how regular their bus into town is or what they think about the state of local schools. It's all politics.

Whether you are a big state socialist or a small state libertarian, it is hard to argue that we do not all have a say – and a responsibility – to care about our local area and the state of the services which are provided. To opt not to have your say into this process seems a bit daft.

Making laws and making parliaments are like

sausages – you want a decent end product, you want to enjoy it even though you know it can be disappointing once you get stuck in, but you don't want to see them getting made. Politics is messy, full of gristle and can be unsatisfactory but you live in hope that in the end it will all be worth it.

People often describe politics as *'tribal'* but actually I think the genuine issue is that in our modern world we find it too easy not to understand someone else's normality. What might be *'normal'* for me may not be *'normal'* for you, and vice versa.

You would think that being born in Buckinghamshire and having grown up in Hertfordshire, that my normality would be a traditional English Home Counties' conservative outlook on life. But our worldview is not simply dependent on where we live or where we were born – though in most cases this is the biggest contributing factor.

Undoubtedly, we get a lot of our hang-ups, views and prejudices passed onto us without us even knowing, from an early age. Usually this is from the things our parents say and do, though it is unlikely they will ever talk to us about politics in the established sense. Because no-one has tried to deliberately indoctrinate us, we then believe that this worldview is probably the same as everyone else around us, though in reality the range of views will be diverse in nature. Too often people believe that their neighbours or political opponents take an opposing view point because they are either not looking at all the facts or that they are misunderstanding the situation – they don't generally consider that the person opposite them may have a totally different set of life experiences informing their opinion.

I used to have a geography teacher at school who would rail about how bad the trade unions were and how wonderful Margaret Thatcher was. I remember a conversation we had in the mid-90s, it went something like this:

"Margaret Thatcher is the greatest politician this country has ever seen – aside from Winston Churchill, obviously. She really sorted those trade unions out. That's why we need the Conservatives back in."

"You're history."

"No, I'm geography."

"Don't change the subject."

"Do you not remember the Winter of Discontent?!"

"No."

"Oh. Well it was bad."

My teacher could not understand how anyone could not support the Conservatives following what happened in the Winter of Discontent. What he hadn't bargained on was that there would be people voting at the next General Election who had not been born during the Winter of Discontent (or even if we had been born, we would have been too small to remember anything about it).

I can see the same argument being made in reverse on social media up and down the country at the moment.

"You can't vote Conservative."

"Why not?"

"Don't you remember Thatcher?"

"No. I wasn't born."

For a generation who have known nothing pre-Tony Blair, why would they vote as a reaction to periods of government that passed long before they were even on the planet?

But, as I say, we pick things up from our parents.

My own Mum and Dad were from differing backgrounds, but I am sure each had their own effect on my political outlook.

Dad grew up in Wigan. A mining town that during the 80s and 90s was run into the ground by the ruling Conservative administrations.

If someone had said *"What's jobs like in Wigan?" "It's the pits"* would have been an accurate response. My Grandad was a pit worker and a union organiser. Low wages, high risks and low life expectancy meant that when this only chance of meaningful employment was removed, unemployment went through the roof.

They talk of towns being company towns, but then what do you do if the company shuts down? Wigan wasn't owned by a company, its industry was state run and then the state washed their hands of it destroying entire communities into the bargain.

When my Dad was a boy, the kids used to walk the streets on election day singing this song about Labour candidate Ronnie Williams (it is sung to the tune of *'Go Tell It On The Mountain'*):

*"Vote, vote, vote for Ronnie Williams,
He's the man who's going to win.
If you don't vote for him,
We'll kick your windows in,
Cos Ronnie is the greatest in the land."*

Fortunately, for the most part, political campaigning has changed for the better since then, but you can see that it was culturally accepted if you were a true Wiganer you were not going to vote anything but Labour, if you had any sense.

My Mum grew up on the Isle of Man. The way politics works over there is that someone comes around to your house and says: *"My Grandad knew your Grandad"*. You do a special handshake and, thanks very much, that's that.

But let's not focus on Manx politics. 1) It is outside the UK 2) It's not very interesting.

As adults, my Dad worked his entire life on the railways – he did not get a great salary, but did get free rail travel, which is both a blessing and a curse. My Mum worked part-time as an optician. As a result, we didn't have much money growing up.

Growing up in South West Hertfordshire when you don't have much money is tough. Not only are you fighting poverty, you are surrounded by great affluence. There are more millionaires in places like Chorleywood and Moor Park than there are anywhere else, outside of Surrey. There's a stigma attached to that, obviously, but all I can remember is not having enough money to go on holiday, not having a car and not being able to buy new shoes. At primary school I can remember entire terms of wearing shoes too small for me, and hitting secondary school needing trainers for P.E. and having a total budget of £12 to spend on this (most of my contemporaries were wearing sports shoes 10 times this in value). You get used to it, but you never forget.

But it's not tribal. I don't hate rich people just because they are rich. It is not inverted snobbery. I only dislike it when people who have no understanding of poverty talk to me about things like *"skivers vs strivers"* or people at the bottom of society being there because they *"are not trying hard enough"*.

We currently have a Government headed by men who not only went to private prep schools and independent fee paying schools, then went to Oxbridge Universities and were members of the most elitist clubs whilst studying there. Some are even members of the aristocracy. Do I hate them for this privilege? No. Do I hate them because they are better off than us and have not had to work their way from the bottom? No. Am I frustrated that they have not had to engage with the mainstream through most of their lives growing up? Yes, but this for them is normal. This is their upbringing. You can not hate a person for being born into the wrong family. What I do object to is the rhetoric and dogmatic policy-making based around a total misunderstanding of those in poverty and those dependent on public services.

Politicians, of whatever hue, have a responsibility to base their decisions around facts and statistical analysis. They should not be trying to make stats fit their predetermined expectations.

So, yet again, we have a party trying to dismantle public services and the welfare state because they see it as a drain on finances, rather than something that is in place to help those who require this assistance. We pay our taxes for a reason, because the Government (or local authorities, depending on the services) has a responsibility to ensure things like a decent level of education for all, or decent healthcare for all or safe and secure communities that are subject to the rule of law.

"For hardworking people" is the slogan – totally ignoring two key facts. 1) Many people who are well-off in this country did not amass their fortunes through hard work – they

inherited them from their forefathers or by accident of birth 2) The vast majority of people in poverty in this country are hardworking – 6 out of 10 families in poverty in the UK have at least one adult in work - this is not about people *'choosing'* to be unemployed for a *'lifestyle on benefits'*, this is about hard-working low-paid workers not being paid a Living Wage to support their families and then being told that the tax credits they are dependent on are being removed because they are a bind on society in tough economic times.

My politics has always been informed by my upbringing and by my faith. We have a moral duty to care for the poor and vulnerable – when we instead try to use them as scapegoats for the failing economy, we have real issues. I am sorry but when we see political parties trying to turn the low paid in on each other, I wonder if that truly benefits anyone. We are going through a global economic downturn caused by highly paid bankers, who received massive bonuses whilst gambling our financial security away – to listen to some politicians and their friends in the media, you would think that the perilous financial situation was instead caused by feral working classes choosing to live on benefits whilst the rest of us go out to work to pay for their giant TVs and X Boxes, and by opportunist immigrants. Our politics needs intellectual and factual rigour if we are to ever take it seriously.

This reminds me of a Polish family I used to see in Manchester when I caught the bus to work. They would let everyone else onto the bus first – helping anyone with bags or buggies in the process, and would say hello to everyone and ask them how they were. They would drop the kids at school, and – as they were dressed in office clothing, I presume they went to their jobs in the city centre. When I came home of an evening, the mother was then on her way out to work a second job in a local restaurant.

I mentioned this to a colleague, who said: *"Bloody Eastern Europeans, coming over here, being polite, working hard and paying their taxes."*

Instead of looking for the things that unite us, too often politics is about finding what can drive us apart. Political rhetoric and oratory is too often based around pressing buttons that will make people go out and vote in a particular way, rather than delivering us a healthier and happier society.

Don't get me wrong, I am equally annoyed and frustrated when I see a Labour Party run by people privately-educated politicians with names like *'Harriet'* and *'Tristan'* talking about years of oppression to hard working people. The question, which I will come to later in this book, is how do we make the political process genuinely more representative of the country we all live in.

I rather fell into working in politics. I studied hard at school, I got decent GCSEs and A-Levels. Then I went to University and got a decent degree and expected to walk into any job I wanted. No-one had prepared me for the fact that the reality of the job market is very different for ordinary people.

I spent 6 months unemployed – though I didn't claim unemployment benefit during this period, I lived off the little money I had saved up through working in my teenage years and a small amount of pocket money. Every day I would apply for around a dozen jobs in various fields and with various salaries.

Through the entire period I think I had 4 job interviews – one of which was at the Job Centre, where I was told I did not have the skills or experience to work as temporary Christmas till cover for Virgin Megastore. It's moments like this which can kill your optimism.

If you do not have a vocational degree, or hands-on job experience, it is difficult to get a look in. I found it hard to get companies to even reply to my emails/phone calls/applications. The same is true at the moment with around 1 million young people unemployed in the UK – listening to the rhetoric you'd think these people spend their entire lives playing video games, drinking strong lager and eating takeaways on your money – actually what most people need is practical assistance into the jobs market and not to be treated like a social leper into the bargain. The latest wheeze is a plan to put the young unemployed into community service – as if they have commited the social crime of being young during an economic downturn. Make them sign on every day at the job centre and then go out and pick up litter or paint graffiti-ed walls in their spare time. Why they don't just make them wear a sign round their necks that says *"Unemployed – Kick Me"*, I don't know.

Having missed my preferred choice of university by one grade (I got B, C, C in my A-Levels rather than B, B, C) instead of going to Warwick to become a primary school teacher (with 100% record of getting students into employment following graduation), I ended up in Cambridge studying English and Politics.

Before you get excited about my Oxbridge education, I should point out I went to university at Anglia Polytechnic University – the only polytechnic by name in the whole country, and it was there on merit.

The name was always a problem. At some point, the name had been changed from Cambridge College of Arts and Technology (CCAT) and then they had had real problems changing it to anything else.

For obvious reasons, they couldn't call it *'Cambridge University'* and *'Anglia University'* was out due to their already being a *'University of East Anglia'* in existence. Most of my undergrad life seemed to be answering surveys about what we might like to change the name to. It never made any difference. One term, so hacked off with the whole experience, we tried to get them to change it to *'Emmanuel College, Cambridge'*, that went down like a proverbial lead balloon. It would be many years after we left that they finally changed the name to *'Anglia Ruskin University'*...after Patron John Ruskin...er...yes. If you look at the signs on Cambridge railway station though you will see that they all say: *"Welcome to Cambridge – Home of Anglia Ruskin University"*. I am guessing this is part of some advertising agreement, rather than any genuine attempt to recognise the cultural and educational importance of the old poly – but maybe things are different now.

The university itself has allegedly been immortalised on TV twice, as far as I am aware. Once when Griff Rhys Jones played a failed lecturer in *Wilt*. (Apparently writer Tom Sharpe based the book, and subsequent film, around the time he was a lecturer at the university – and popular rumour has it that the incident with a blow up doll and one of the academic staff was based more in fact than it was in fiction.)

The second time was when *The Young Ones* appeared as *'Scumbag College'* against the fictional Oxbridge institution of *'Footlights College'*. I say allegedly on both counts, as both times the name of the institution was cleverly altered in order to not welcome a lawsuit from eager lawyers.

Don't get me wrong, I loved my university years. The lecturers were great, the courses were brilliant and the staff were always friendly and accommodating. There were no pretensions and my university years were undoubtedly some of the best of my life.

But the one thing that let it down was admin. Well admin and organisation – two things. A two week wait for a timetable was not unusual in my day. I can remember in 1995, my first year at university, that one student did not get his timetable till week 6. Now that may sound quite bad, but it is worth remembering that at that time we had 12 week terms!

So maybe I should not have been that surprised at the dearth of offers when I threw myself into the jobs market. Though, having said that, famous Tory Party donor Lord Michael Ashcroft went to Anglia back in the day and it never did him any harm. In fact, he has been Chancellor of Anglia Ruskin University since November 2001, and has donated £5 million for the university's business school at Chelmsford, now called Ashcroft International Business School. I am guessing he didn't study a BA Hons in English and Politics though.

When our university newspaper had the big splash *"Anglia Polytechnic - Biggest Drinkers in UK"* most of us thought this was a boast, rather than social commentary about the state of our livers. That's the way we rolled.

But find a job I eventually did. Pulling pints in Wetherspoons. I got on their fast-track management scheme, but lasted two days. I had asked for either Saturdays or Sundays off so I could go to Church (I was playing in a Christian football team on the Saturday doing practical mission work, so either would have suited me). I was told that was fine through the interview process and then told at the signing the contract stage that this was not fine. I refused to sign the contract and went home dejected. I'd spent 6 months waiting for a job to spring up and then when one finally did, I had turned it down. I began questioning my reasoning.

That evening, I was contacted by two separate people about a job in politics working for an MP. Neither had spoken to each other about it. One had heard the MP speaking at a conference that day and the second had heard through a Christian organisation that the MP was recruiting and looking for someone with a faith.

Within a week, I had the job.

The Christian organisation in question was the Christian Socialist Movement (CSM) – which is, in short, the Labour Party's Christian affiliate (although now it has been renamed *'Christians on the Left'* in a blatant attempt to not give the impression it might be a bunch of unreformed Marxists. This has mainly only upset the people who *are* unreformed Marxists).

The Director of CSM lived 5 minutes away from my house and I popped around for a coffee. They were looking for a Christian, interested in the political process, with a left of centre perspective. It was perfect for me and perfect for them – I hoped it would be perfect for the MP too. A few days later I was interviewed in Parliament by the MP, his wife and the Director for CSM. We talked mostly about football and rugby, and my background, rather than anything too job specific. It seemed too good to be true.

Looking back, you could say it was no different to the old school tie network; or that it was coincidence, simply being in the right place at the right time; or that it was a God determined event that was meant to be. I will let you all decide for yourself which you think is more likely – but the long and short of it is that I ended up working in Parliament.

2. Working In Parliament

You may be forgiven for thinking that working in Parliament is an extremely glamorous experience. After all, we have been brought up to believe that London is the centre of the known universe. However, what any (non-Thatcherite) geography teacher will tell you is that London is not even in the centre of the UK.

It is no real surprise that our national psyche is London-centric, after all it is our national capital and, by population has more residents than anywhere else. For example, there are more people living in London than in the whole of Scotland, or Wales, or Northern Ireland.

However this has meant that our political classes can often become quite blinkered to what is happening outside the Westminster bubble. Is it any wonder that people feel let down by a system where many MPs see Birmingham as *'up North'* and the furthest they will have travelled up the country is when they went to university in the northern hotspots of Cambridge or Oxford?

It doesn't help that our civil service is increasingly centralised – pressures on budgets meaning it is deemed cheaper to move everybody back in-house to offices in Whitehall, rather than having them work out in regional hubs. In the late 1990s there was a push for more regionalism, more self-determination, more devolution – for the most part, economically and with regard to broadening national esteem, it was a great success, even if we did get H'Angus the Monkey as Mayor of Hartlepool for two terms.

I will always remember waking up and hearing a North Eastern voice on the radio announcing: *"My name is Stuart Drummond. I am not a monkey. The monkey is behind me."* It sounded like a clever metaphor for life which we should all adopt, though sadly Stuart meant it in a more literal sense.

H'Angus, mascot of Hartlepool United Football Club, managed to unite the protest vote in a town which clearly had had its fill of politicians at that time. His one electoral policy was to introduce free bananas to school children, though when elected he was unable to fulfil this commitment due to budget constraints. Welcome to politics, Stuart. It could have been worse, the original Hartlepool monkey was summarily executed by the navy because they suspected he might be a French spy. No, really.

They said the 1980s was a great time to be a singer, a writer, a poet, a comedian. What they meant was, it was a terrible time to be a singer, writer, poet, comedian or anyone from outside South East England but it did mean that the feeling of injustice meant you wrote some fantastic stuff in response to your social situation.

I worry when I hear politicians genuinely advocate that we should stop putting money into areas like Middlesbrough or Hull and instead *"put investment into areas which are more successful"* – surely we have a responsibility not to turn our backs on whole communities, sending out a message we do not value them? I wonder how many of these politicians have actually been to Middlesbrough or Hull – I can tell you I have, and there are some fantastic vibrant communities full of people who have a lot to contribute to our nation.

More recently, we had a Government Minister (an Economic Secretary to the Treasury, no less) tell a part-time worker in Bolton that there were plenty of jobs near her and that she should go and get employment in a car factory in Sunderland.

For any Economic Secretaries to the Treasury out there reading this, it is worth pointing out that Sunderland is 143 miles from Bolton. I've heard of *'getting on your bike'* to find work, but that is ridiculous. If the lady had have taken such a job, the journey would take two-and-a-half hours to drive – or four hours on the train – and the same coming back every single day. Goodness how long it would take on a push-bike.

I can only imagine the costs involved with such a daily commute, but I can empathise with losing a big chunk of your salary in travel pay.

When I started my new job in Parliament, I was on a salary of £9,000 a year. I was meant to be working 4 days for the MP in his Parliamentary office and 1 day across the road helping the Christian Socialist Movement with their work.

Before I had earned a penny, I had to pay for a rail ticket to get me from near Watford into Central London. The cost of this was around £1,400. I was fortunate that I could take a loan from my parents, but I am sure most people may not be so fortunate. Indeed when you look at all the interns working for free in Parliament, you have to accept the only people who are really able to do this are people who live in Central London, or those that can afford to do an unpaid placement for a long period of time (i.e. people who already have some level of independent means).

It is worth saying that my arrival, though it did post-date decimalisation, was before the advent of Minimum Wages and campaigns for interns to get fair wages for their work. Sadly, interns were often free disposable labour, with a long cue of potential interns behind them ready to take on the work if they were not up to scratch.

£9,000 may seem like a pittance, but I was grateful for the opportunity. The average wage at that time for MPs' staff was £7,000 a year – so it wasn't as if I felt I had too much to complain about.

The problem with the way MPs' offices are funded is that there is no central HR unit or department that ensures best employment practice is followed. The budgets for staffing are universally seen as being too low – however each individual MP has a limited budget, and journalists lazily describe things such as employees as *'expenses'*. Any push for raising staffing budgets is seen as an attempt for MPs to line their own pockets – and several stories will be written about the MPs who employ their own family as staff. (Yes, this does happen, but it is not a reason for denying the vast majority at least a Living Wage.)

The trade unions, and the rather more grand Secretaries & Assistants Council (the purple corduroy trouser and floral dress wearing brigade who would rather self-combust than join a trade union) pushed for recognised job descriptions and titles with standard salaries, which was eventually delivered, however limited budgets mean that these are generally not adhered to. You will see most job adverts to work for MPs say *"Salary in line with Parliamentary Pay Scales"* – loosely translated, this means *"Whatever I have left in my staffing budget"*.

Another problem with this approach is that many MPs will have no experience of running a department, managing budgets or managing staff. This means that the demands put on staff can be outside standard employment practices – and it does keep the trade union representatives busy.

One MP, who I shan't name, used to get through staff/interns at the rate of a couple a month due to his frequent tantrums – one particular one resulted in the lead member of his office getting a stapler around the back of the head. Another MP replaced a key member of her staff and appointed the American intern he had been training – which although keeping costs down in the short-term does leave you liable to action being taken.

As a junior member of staff it is difficult to know what you can and cannot do. You just hope you won't be exploited. Every single Parliamentary Assistant or Researcher does a slightly different job depending on who their employer is and what their particular demands are. It would be better to have a centralised system with standard job descriptions, pay and conditions to ensure staff are protected and that MPs can rely on a professional service. Will it happen? I doubt it.

Parliament is a confusing place at the best of times. When you come out of Westminster tube station – a station which has won architectural prizes for looking remarkably like the Industrial Zone from the Crystal Maze – you are directly in the shadow of Big Ben.

Before anyone says it, I know Big Ben actually refers to the main bell rather than the tower. I've done the tour. I've stood behind the clock faces. I've got the T-shirt* (*I haven't actually got a Big Ben T-shirt). It's actually the St Stephen's Tower – or as it was renamed for Her Majesty The Queen's Diamond Jubilee, The Elizabeth Tower.

Either way, this tower is towering and impressive. On my first day as I crossed the road (before the days of the *'secret'* underground passage between Portcullis House and the Houses of Parliament's main buildings), I stood next to Neil Kinnock. *"Wow"*, I thought, *"one day I may stand next to someone vaguely important on this crossing...but clearly not today."*

It reminds me of when a non-political friend came to visit me in Parliament and we stumbled upon William Hague (the then Leader of the Conservative Party) in a Parliamentary reception. He said: *"Is that William Hague? Really?! You wouldn't expect to see him here!"* Which made me wonder where would you expect to see the Leader of the Opposition, if not in Parliament?

The Palace of Westminster is a warren. Inevitably you will get lost, but don't worry, there will be someone to shout at you if you are in the wrong place at the wrong time. There are certain places you are allowed to go; certain places you are not allowed to go; and then certain places you aren't allowed to go, but you are allowed to go at certain specified times. That last one is totally random, like when there's an *'R'* in the month or at Church when something happens on the second Tuesday of the month (unless it's a 5 week month, in which case it will be held on a Wednesday in the small hall). You get the idea. There are rules about rules in Westminster and it is impossible to learn them all – even if you did learn them all, they would probably then change the rules to keep you on your toes.

The people employed to keep you on your toes are the Serjeant at Arms. Not the scary Parliamentary police with machine guns, but the men and ladies dressed in tights and ornate ruffs – they will usually be carrying a ceremonial stick too, just in case their garb didn't instantly tell you they were important.

For many years they were led by a man named Sir Peter Grant Peterkin. This tells you much of what you need to know about the assembled ranks of be-tighted minions, most of whom are ex-forces. I keenly await the Mel Brookes production of *Serjeant at Arms: Men In Tights* starring Peter Grant Peterkin, but as yet it hasn't happened.

There are three main times you will come into contact with the Serjeant at Arms: 1) If you are an MP, these are the people who will give you some snuff and pass notes around for you in the Parliamentary Chamber – as if you were still at some old fashioned public school for naughty boys (which is probably exactly what the Parliamentary authorities intended to ensure some semblance of order); 2) If you need to move offices. Although the main decisions over accommodation come down to the relevant party Whips Offices, and their *'Accommodation Whip'* – i.e. the scariest, most unmovable of all the scary unmovable whips – the Serjeant at Arms ensure that the offices are distributed fairly and proportionately. This stops the party in power having all the nice offices and those in Opposition parties being stuck in the shoe box offices with no natural light. Reshuffles don't only change ministerial or shadow ministerial line-ups, they also ensure a big reshuffle of offices – where numerous MPs suddenly call in to see if they might want to nab your office once you've gone. You may feel like shouting *"I'm not dead yet, leave me be!"* but you know sooner or later Kirstie Allsopp will make a programme for Channel 4 about this whole process; 3) When dealing with matters of security, such as fires or fracas.

Our first Parliamentary Office was in the Norman Shaw Buildings. This is where Old Scotland Yard was based, before the move a few hundred yards up the road – this is where the investigations into crimes committed by

Jack The Ripper and others would have been conducted. There is a certain feeling of jail cell chic about it.

Apparently the Norman Shaw Buildings are red sandstone because during the Blitz the authorities didn't want Luftwaffe bombers to be able to spot the buildings against the London skyline. They perhaps forgot that the capital's streets were dirty black and not red like the surface of Mars when coming to this conclusion, but at least there was some reasoning for these buildings being totally incongruous with the surrounding area.

Our first office was a tiny *'L-shaped'* ground floor office in Norman Shaw North where you could not see the MP from your own desk. After a couple of years, we got promoted to the floor above, to an office which was equally small, but did have a balcony. The representative from the Serjeant at Arms office advised us not to go out onto the balcony or leave the window open, as this was a security risk. When asked what this *'security risk'* might be, he looked a bit confused and that stuttered: *"Well, a sniper could shoot you from over there"*. Over there referred to the other side of the Thames, towards County Hall and eventually to where the London Eye would be constructed. To be honest, while I appreciate the words of caution, if someone is prepared to travel half way up the London Eye or the Saatchi Gallery in the off-chance I might open the window a little bit in order to take a head shot, then they are welcome to do so. Fair play, you have to admire that level of commitment to the cause, but there are much easier ways to kill me.

Security in Parliament is rightly tight. Every one of the buildings on the Parliamentary Estate has *'bomb proof'* curtains. It should be pointed out though that these curtains would not actually protect you if someone put a bomb directly against it, what they are are heavy curtains with lead weights in the bottom, which would catch any flying glass if there was an explosion in the general vicinity.

The neighbouring office to us on the first floor of Norman Shaw North was a massive suite. The occupant of this suite changed variously. Sometimes it was occupied by a high ranking former Conservative Minister, sometimes it was a Conference Room facility for Parliamentary meetings and for some of the time it was an office for a rather 'eccentric' back bench MP who would tell us he loved our bookshelves and this is why we were *"winning the war"*. Whether he was referring to the war in Iraq, the political war for the hearts and minds of the British public at the ballot box, or the Second World War, I have absolutely no idea. What I do know is that his giant room had one sofa in the middle, a single table in the corner with a chair and a giant haemorrhoid ball within it. This is probably why he was not *"winning the war"*.

The office block was mixed between Members and staff of all the major political parties. Boris Johnson had an office a few doors down, which was always entertaining when he was doing MP duties rather than editing The Spectator. Who knew then what glories lay ahead for him!

I enjoyed being in this political backwater and it was not until many years later we would hit the rarefied heights of obtaining an office in Portcullis House.

Portcullis House is a state of the art development, which cost over £1 million per MP that had an office within it. It caused a ruckus when it was developed. Many backbench MPs signed Early Day Motions (the Parliamentary equivalent of a petition to the Headmaster, but with less effectiveness and power than that) and bravely spoke out to say they would not be accepting an office in this ginormous white elephant which was an affront to modern democracy and the ordinary everyday people of the UK – safe in the knowledge they were never going to be offered a place in this plush pad for up and coming stars and former Cabinet Ministers. A few years on, many would be happily accepting keys to their new offices in this part of the Estate.

Portcullis House is easy to spot. Next to the train station, on the corner of Westminster Bridge and the Embankment, it resembles a giant greenhouse. If you can imagine a larger version of the Crystal Dome from the end game of the Crystal Maze then you will have it exactly right.

I imagine any new development in the middle of Westminster would be pricey at the best of times, but there was concern expressed at the cost of the tree-lined atrium inside the building (apparently the trees could have been purchased at a fraction of the cost at most local garden centres) and the running water tables (which spent as much time switched off as on due to them repeatedly leaking down onto the underground station directly below them).

Also there were numerous fire alarms due to the fire/smoke sensors being directly above the kitchens. This was a modern variation on a theme, in Norman Shaw North we would repeatedly be evacuated due to policemen wafting talc around in the shower rooms at the top of the building. Apparently talc confuses smoke detectors – which is good to know.

I still have no idea why policemen choose to waft talc around each other, but it led to a series of big signs in large print from Serjeant at Arms telling people not to waft talc in the showers. Talc wafting is another serious issue that comes under their portfolio of powers.

This predated the incident where some Fathers For Justice protesters threw purple talc at Tony Blair from Strangers' Gallery in the House of Commons, so maybe there was a germ of prescience in their directives. Interestingly, if that purple talc had been ricin or another toxic poison we would have probably all died as, instead of following established procedure of locking down the Chamber with the MPs and the poison gas inside, the authorities simply allowed the MPs to walk back to their offices spreading the noxious substance with them. We have to accept that MPs are the important ones and the rest of us are just collateral damage.

Normally when there is a fire alarm, a recorded announcement from one of the now retired Serjeant at Arms goes out. The clipped tones state the following: *"There is a far in your aria. Please evacuate the building immediately."* Most of us then wonder what a far would be doing in an aria and what that means for those of us who have never been to an opera. By the time we work out that this is posh talk for *"There is a fire in your area"* we would all have been burnt to a crisp if it was a genuine fire alert. I suspect it may be a conspiracy to cut down the amount of working-class people in Parliament.

The other notable thing that happens when the fire alarm sounds is that all the walls in the corridors of Portcullis House move to block your exit. The reason this happens is to compartmentalise any fire or smoke, and you must push the wall to escape to a stairwell. Unfortunately, at the best of times, it is difficult to locate walls and doors in Portcullis House. Whilst staff offices have frosted glass doors, most offices of MPs are made of wood panelling that looks exactly the same as the wood panelled walls of the corridors. This has led to several incidents of researchers leaning against what they thought was a wall, only to end up on the floor of an MP's private office with the startled VIP stood directly over them. You have no chance during a fire alarm when these walls move 90 degrees in one or other direction – it just adds weight to my theory that it is all a conceit and that Portcullis House is not actually an office block for MPs, rather it is a Channel 5 remake of the Crystal Maze in early production.

When I finally moved on from Portcullis House and relocated to the Lower Ministerial Corridor, in the very centre of Parliament, I wondered what manner of new-fangled gadgets may be ahead of me – but interestingly these rooms are the starkest, bleakest rooms you will ever encounter, like a punishment room from a Cold War era Communist State. Consistently dark with no windows or outside light to break the gloom, all you can hear is the slow drip-drip of water coming from somewhere. You're best off not asking where, what or why. Conspiracy theorists might suggest this is an attempt to keep those with genuine power in check, but actually all it really does is keep their researchers in woollen jumpers for most of the year.

Thankfully it is rare that there is a genuine security incident. Yes, there was that time when Bryan Ferry's son – and a bunch of his fox hunt supporting friends – broke into the House of Commons Chamber and did some serious finger-wagging but aside from that we seem to have got by OK.

I worked in Parliament during the unfolding tragedy of September 11th. We watched it on our TV screens, unsure if we would be next. Later that week we were all hurried outside due to an alarm, and to be honest, there was a real sense of fear and trepidation.

For around an hour or so, we all huddled outside nervously looking at the planes flying overhead and trying not to stand too near any parked cars. We were then all told it was safe to return to work.

Worried that there had been some sort of serious security breach, we asked one of the Serjeant at Arms staff what had been the nature of the alarm.

"Some plonker burnt some toast in one of the kitchen areas", came the terse reply. I suspect he then went off to draw up a *'Burnt Toast'* missive.

During the 7/7 attacks, despite Parliament being a possible target for bombers, I walked miles in order to reach the Estate as once inside it is the probably the safest place in the country. Full lockdowns are few and far between. Someone will explain to me why staff and their property is thoroughly searched at times like these, but MPs and Lords are exempted from these little annoyances. I presume because of their breeding, they would never dare commit the faux pas of supporting terrorism – even the ones who previously belonged to the political wings of terrorist groups.

Rumour has it that, as it is a Royal Palace, the Palace of Westminster is exempted from the laws of the land. Whether that is to do with health and safety or employment law or anything else you can think of. I suspect in practice the rule of law is followed in the vast majority of cases, but it's a nice talking point when showing tourists around the building. It certainly doesn't stop the *'Health and Safety mindset'* – the total risk aversion that corporate bodies have nowadays in our litigious society. One autumnal afternoon I saw a Parliamentary Works Department employee handpicking leaves from the trees outside Members' Entrance – I presume this was in case the leaves fell on anyone, or in case anyone slipped on the leaves whilst they were lying on the ground. All I know is that it was bordering on overkill, especially when you reflect that in Members' Cloakroom (next to the Members' Entrance) MPs have a ribbon on their clothes peg from which to hang their sword – and there is a Parliamentary shooting gallery underneath the Palace where those who like such things can discharge their mechanised weapons into a paper target or two.

Members' Entrance is famous for a couple of reasons: 1) Unlike many of the security points on the Estate there is no snuff stored here, but there is a special bell to summon taxis to pick up MPs. Everywhere in Parliament has *'Members' Priority Service'* whether you are buying lunch, hailing taxis or buying chocolate and teddies as a Christmas present for friends and family – it is interesting to see which MPs actually enforce this archaic privilege though, most are too embarrassed to; 2) Just a few feet away is the site of the first traffic light ever installed in the UK – gas powered, it was erected on 10th December 1868 but was removed under a month later when it exploded and killed the policeman stood under it. Traffic lights were therefore abandoned until the much safer electric version could be invented years later; 3) The green area in front of Members' Entrance is not only where David Blunkett exercises his guide dog, but it is also directly above a big multi-story car park that is reserved for the use of MPs. This area is where Airey Neave was blown up by the INLA in 1979 in a car bomb attack as he left the car park.

Another popular rumour is that if you were to die within the Parliamentary Estate that you would be entitled to a state funeral, due to this being a Royal Palace. Again, it is unclear whether this is actually true, but the accepted practice is for those in a grievous condition to be transferred immediately to St Thomas' Hospital which lies on the other side of Westminster Bridge. Those who are already deceased are then declared *'Dead On Arrival'*. I am aware of several occasions where this has happened, but to use the tragic example of Neave, following the attack his body was apparently taken to St Thomas' in two separate ambulances and his death certificate at the hospital was marked *'DOA'*.

I shouldn't give the impression that Parliament is an unfriendly or unwelcoming place. Any UK citizen is entitled to come to Parliament at any time to lobby their MP (though you would be well advised to contact them in advance if you actually want them to be there to meet you!). Coming through the main public entrance at St Stephen's Entrance, you will be directed to Central Lobby – past the point where Prime Minister Spencer Percival was *"assassinated by a madman"* and from there you can wait whilst a *'green card'* is issued. This does not mean that anything happens to your immigration status, rather that someone on reception fills out a green piece of card with your contact details on and tries to track down your MP. Sadly this practice predates most modern technologies and often, rather than phone the relevant MP's office, the member of staff will physically try and find the MP or put the card on the MPs' Message Board in Members' Lobby – which is not especially useful if they are not in or going through Members' Lobby at that time. If this is the case, then the card turns up in the office postbag a couple of days later – and you have to hope that the constituent has gone home by this point.

There is a particularly un-politically correct story about the four main doorways leading from Central Lobby. Above each is a picture of a British Patron Saint. Above the entrance to the Commons is St David, the Patron Saint of Wales, this is said to represent the lower house, where the all the talking is done by the commoners. Above the entrance to the Lords is St George, the Patron Saint of England, this is said to represent the Upper House and the Royal end of the building where those who think they are superior to everyone else sit. Above the entrance directly facing you as you walk in is St Andrew, the Patron Saint of Scotland, this route takes you to where all the refreshment facilities are and so you can get yourself a nice relaxing whisky. And finally above the main entrance, which leads back to St Stephen's, is St Patrick, the Patron Saint of Ireland, this is said to be because this is the entrance and exit and the Irish don't know if they are coming or going. I know it sounds like a Bernard Manning routine from The Comedians, but there you go. As someone who has English, Scottish and Irish relatives (sorry, no Welsh family yet, so I can't speak for you) I have to say that whilst it is moderately offensive, it is still quite funny.

Parliament is a bit like a public schoolboy's dream gentleman's club – but hopefully, through time and perseverance, we can make it a bit more accessible, a bit more representative and a bit more normal.

Which brings us very nicely to my next chapter about how it's important to enjoy yourself whilst in Parliament. We are all human after all, some of us just hide it better.

3. Enjoying Yourself In Parliament

The Houses of Parliament is an historic building. It is a living museum, a tourist attraction, a place where laws are made and, in rare cases, a court of law – but it is also a working building.

Over 7,000 people work in Parliament. It should be remembered that not all will be MPs, Lords or their staff. There are chefs, police, administrative staff, librarians, nurses, doctors, fire officers and many others besides. There is even a hairdressers here tucked away by the Terrace Cafeteria.

All of these people work hard to ensure that our Parliament functions the way it should. OK, maybe not the MPs, but the rest of them, certainly.

It's important with so many workers under one roof that there are opportunities to relax and wind down.

For those that work for MPs, the 24/7 demands of a stressful job – managing not only their bosses but the media and often unhappy constituents – means that any window for a short rest is quickly utilised. I know the tabloid media would readily run a campaign, now I have said that, stating that those paid from the public purse should not have a spare second to relax – but as someone who has worked ridiculously long hours for something bordering on a state-sanctioned pittance, I can say that short periods of rest must be embraced for those in highly stressful jobs. If you do not allow this (or encourage this), then what you will get is an unhappy, unwell and stressed workforce, which is no good to anybody!

The most obvious time you will see this manana attitude is on a Friday within Parliament. The ties come off, the Converse boots and jeans come out of the cupboard, and there is much bleary-eyed evidence that suggests the political workhorses stayed up a little too late last night watching Question Time and This Week on BBC1 with a glass of something fortifying.

The reason for this is that Friday is the day that MPs work from their constituencies. Because most MPs do not have constituencies in London, the way the Parliamentary timetable is scheduled means that most can travel down on Monday morning for an afternoon sitting in Westminster, work through Monday to Thursday in the Commons, and then head back to their constituencies late on Thursday.

There is a great misunderstanding about what an MP's work entails. Many think that if the parliamentary Chamber is nearly empty that the MPs are not doing any work. In reality, this is not usually the case.

As well as sitting in on debates, MPs will sit on Standing Committees (though never stand on Sitting Committees); hold meetings with groups, Ministers and NGOs; do casework; reply to correspondence, emails and phone enquiries from their offices; as well as a variety of other commitments. At all times they must be within 8 minutes of the voting lobbies, in case a Division of the House is called. It is unlikely they are off larging it up at China Whites or Stringfellows.

It begs the question of whether MPs should sit in the Chamber constantly, just to give the impression that they are *'working hard'*, whilst ignoring all their other duties and responsibilities to their constituents?

There are always clever ways to try and confuse those watching the live feed of Parliamentary debates at home that turnout is bigger than it is. You will often see when the Adjournment Debate is on something like the economic vibrancy and impact of East Midlands Airport that although there might be under a dozen people in the Chamber, they will all sit huddled together – usually directly behind the main speaker in the debate. This act is called *'doughnutting'*. It is a pretty effective tactic which means that when the local news covers 10 seconds of the debate on their evening coverage, it will look like the Chamber was packed and all those with an interest will see their MP was deeply concerned about this matter, nodding, tutting and hear-hearing from behind to every single comment. This tactic is fatally undermined though if those controlling the cameras go back to a wide shot and show that there are only 8 people in the Chamber, including the Minister who has been forced to respond to the debate.

That's not to say MPs don't like a drink or to go to a nice restaurant of an evening. All I am saying is that they will do so from a safe distance. All the restaurants and bars within Parliament have Division Bells which ring to let MPs know that a division has been called. Even some of the bars, restaurants and shops directly outside Parliament have Division Bells too.

On my first day in Parliament, I nearly jumped out of the window when what I thought was a fire alarm sounded at 2pm. It was a really old-fashioned emergency bell like you used to get at school or on old style fire engines. Everyone else just sat there blindly ignoring this bell and carrying on with their work. It was quite surreal. Little did I know that there was not 'a far in my aria' but rather the House was simply being summoned to the Chamber.

Most of the main parties have embraced technology now though, so as well as a reliance on the bell, they are likely to be instantly messaged on their phones or PDAs. In my day it was pagers and faxes that were cutting edge, but I suspect we are past that now.

In short there are no excuses for missing a vote, and the Whips will be quick to remind you of this. Of an evening, MPs can process numerous times through the Division Lobbies on a series of votes. It is like herding cattle round and round in order to achieve something that nowadays could be completed in seconds via electronic voting. Actually, maybe herding cats is a better analogy than herding cattle.

Also in and around the corridors of Parliament you will see TV sets, these are called *'Annunciators'*. Usually they will be set either to a plain screen telling you what is currently being debated in the Chamber, who the speaker is, when they started speaking and what the actual time is in the real world. At the Commons end of Parliament the screens are green and at the Lords end they are red – and contain the information for that respective Chamber. Each MP has one of these in their office too – Lords do not as under the current system, the vast majority do not get offices, just a locker to keep their stuff in.

What is not known by most is that the majority of these annunciators in the corridors, restaurants and bars will have the sound turned off. This is because every 30 seconds or so a small chime is sounded to remind you that you have left the telly on – it sounds like a small leprechaun playing a harp, and if not muted it will send any normal human mad within 2 minutes. (I suspect there is not actually a small leprechaun inside the annunciator playing a harp, but nothing would surprise me about Parliament anymore.)

Another little known fact is that these annunciators also play a variety of conventional TV and radio to allow MPs to while away the hours waiting for votes to happen. You can get the main terrestrial TV channels, then all the Sky Sports channels, Sky One, the main BBC Radio stations and then a token Welsh language and Scots language channel that nobody watches – and yes, we pay for this privilege. So if you can hear the theme to This Morning blaring out at 10.30 of a morning, coming from an MP's office, you aren't imagining it.

There are several restaurants and bars inside Parliament, many are solely for the use of MPs (or have sections that are solely for the use of MPs). For researchers and assistants the main restaurants of choice are: 1) The Debate Cafeteria (in Portcullis House) serving rather up-market but bijou* (*i.e.

small) helpings of faintly middle class food. Imagine tofu and polenta with a raspberry coulis and you have the idea. This is the *'place to be seen'* if you want to pretend you are a mover and shaker. 2) The Terrace Cafeteria (in the centre of Parliament) serving a wide variety of wholesome food, for every taste, but slightly undone by the fact that you are fairly likely to bump into John Prescott. It is also handily situated next to the gift shop, where you can buy ridiculously overpriced whisky and chocolate when you've run out of half decent things to get your loved ones for Christmas. 3) Bellamy's Cafeteria (in 1 Parliament Street) serving food that would not be out of place in a transport café. Suffice it to say, I love this café and it is my favourite. Good honest food, big portions, friendly staff and no MPs (except the one or two nice ones who like proper food – e.g. Glenda Jackson). This is one of the oldest of the Parliamentary restaurants and is apparently where HP Sauce was invented (this is why it was named Houses of Parliament Sauce and has a picture of the Palace of Westminster on the bottle, even though it is no longer produced in this country).

On a Friday though there are a few other options as the MPs are away and some of the slightly posher outlets are open to the great unwashed – if they book in advance. In my experience though, Parliamentary staff on low wages will inevitably go for the cheaper option – not difficult when most parliamentary meals are heavily subsidised, partly by the charges made to those holding corporate receptions within the Palace – for example, there was a great outcry when the Despatch Box coffee shop in Portcullis House raised the price of a cup of tea from 30p to 35p not so long back.

Too much is made of MPs having *'a day off'* on Fridays. Occasionally there will be Private Members Bills debated on a Friday in Parliament, but (no matter how worthy these may be) these Bills are unlikely to ever become law. Much better for MPs to be back at home serving the people who elected them, listening to their concerns and fears and fighting their corner. Also it gives MPs a chance to see their families. If you are a young MP (i.e someone under the age of 50) you can completely miss your children growing up and spending time with your partner if you are not careful. It is little surprise there are so many affairs when so much time is spent apart, although that doesn't mean we should condone it.

Of course, the Friday feeling is completely reversed if you are a member of an MP's staff working in a constituency office. You spend Monday to Thursday dealing with enquiries from the general public and then your world goes into a spin on Friday as your boss sweeps in and tries to do all the meetings, visits and constituency work he would like to do in one week in one day. Having worked in a constituency office, I can tell you Fridays are fraught. Full of advice surgeries, heated debate and late finishes.

But MPs get great holidays, right? Well, I suppose that depends again on how you define Parliamentary work. It is true to say that there is an extended Summer Recess.

Between the end of July and the beginning of October (usually the second week of October) Parliament is recessed. However this does not mean that the MPs are all off on one giant jolly to Ibiza or wherever. Most MPs will use the Parliamentary recess to undertake a series of local meetings and visits that they would not otherwise be able to fit in. They will also probably use it to network with voters and do leafleting while the weather is good and the days are long. Yes, they will probably take a couple of weeks off in August, but I am not sure we should deny anyone such a luxury.

I get tired of journalists, whose sole job is to sell papers or boost ratings, constantly picking on MPs for things such as how long they go on holiday, and where they go on holiday and what book they might be reading on holiday and how much they are earning whilst being away from the Commons. It would be interesting to do the same for those who work in the media: How much do you earn, where do you go on holiday, how much do you spend on expenses etc etc? I wonder how much they would like that?

I have nothing whatsoever against proper investigative journalism, but when you constantly play to people's fears and the lowest common denominator you have to wonder if it gets us anywhere. I particularly hate faux exposés on *'this person earnt such and such from this company and then asked a question about it!'* Yes, and how do you know about this, because we have a publicly available register of interests where parliamentarians have to declare all their outside earnings and other interests – and then they must declare this orally during debates if asking an associated question. That is not a scandal, that is open democracy. If someone tries to hide payments then that would be a proper scandal worthy of exposure, but what you have done is skimmed through the Register of Interests and then repeated it as if you have actually done some work.

More interesting is to ask why we have such a long Parliamentary Recess. Believe it or not, we owe this to *'The Great Stink of 1858'*, a time when the poor sewerage around Westminster meant that in the heat of Summer raw faeces in and around the Thames would spread fatal diseases such as cholera to those present, including the law makers. As a result it was safer to send the MPs away to their constituencies during the hotter summer months than to have them catching diseases and causing by-elections. For good or ill, the tradition has stuck.

Parliament during the long recess is a completely different world. Partly it is like one long Friday, with staff wearing jeans, making the most of the restaurants they would not normally be allowed near, and in some cases being allowed to eat their lunch outside on the Terrace that overlooks the Thames. I always wonder whether all the tourists waving from the boats going past during the Summer months know they are looking at a bunch of researchers chatting about Hollyoaks rather than a bunch of MPs discussing how we address the national debt.

Long staff lunches are inevitably cut short by people claiming they have a really important piece of work to do, when in reality we know they are rushing back to watch Neighbours or Diagnosis Murder on their office annunciator. I tended to resist such distractions, but I would occasionally put on the cricket or football, if England were playing. This was a slightly odd experience, especially if outside days of recess because you could end up syncing your toilet visits with other people you wouldn't normally chat to. For example, one Conservative MP who is very into his sport, would always watch the cricket whilst doing his work – and we would end up meeting up several times a day in the loos passing pleasantries. Goodness only knows what the other people on a corridor thought we were doing constantly ducking out to the toilet together.

It is at this juncture that I must make a confession that, during Summer Recess, we may have occasionally played office cricket with our co-workers in our office. When we were in Portcullis House, we had two offices next to each other – one for 4 members of staff and one for the MP. If you opened the connecting door, you had a perfect batting wicket for one person to bowl from the end of one office through to the person batting at the other end of the other office. We put two bins on top of each other for the stumps and had a couple of stress balls that had been sent to us by external charities raising awareness of their causes (we even had one that looked like an apple with a mini stalk which allowed some vicious spin bowling to be undertaken).

I wouldn't say we played often, but we did devise our own scoring system and one of my colleagues did create his own bat out of various cardboard tubes (which had contained corporate calendars) and gaffer tape. Before anyone tries to make a party political point out of this, I should say that the players in our games came from across the parties. It was great fun, but there was always a danger that one of Serjeant at Arms men in tights may appear at any moment at the frosted glass and have a few choice words for you. However the only cricketing incident within Parliament I am aware of happened when one of the MPs, in a game unconnected to our own and in a different building, bowling the ball to himself in a corridor took out an annunciator. It transpired that the MP was playing on his own, with a real cricket ball and cricket bat, and denied he had caused the breakage until it was pointed out that the whole incident had been captured on CCTV.

The banter and camaraderie in Parliament is second to none. In a highly stressful, highly competitive environment it is important to have friends you can rely on for support, insight and straight-talking.

During most of my time in Parliament, I shared an office with a big bald-headed Scouser called Dr Dave. Dr Dave was originally from Bootle, and headed up the

Parliamentary work of The Bible Society. He arranged all the prayer times and services for the Christians in Parliament Group (previously the Parliamentary Christian Fellowship) which brought all the MPs, Lords and staff together to worship and study together.

There is a vibrant Christian community within Parliament and it crosses party lines. Every week there will be prayer meetings, every month worship services and plenty of one-off events in between.

Each of the main political parties has a Christian affiliate or grouping. The Conservative Christian Fellowship is probably the best resourced and most influential of them all – money can't buy success, but it does help; Labour has the Christian Socialist Movement – now renamed Christians on the Left because arguably it is no longer Christian, Socialist or much of a Movement; and the Lib Dems have the Liberal Democrat Christian Forum, which is run by someone on a part-time basis. Rather than promote ideology, these separate groupings normally exist to help encourage Christians to become more involved in the political process. Good on them for that.

Being in communion with people of vastly differing views and backgrounds is always entertaining. I can remember one lunch time when a Conservative researcher brayed about how she was going to her estate at the weekend for the shooting. Dr Dave, quick as a flash, said: *"Yeah, we had some shooting on our estate – but I think the police have got a hold of it now"*. Needless to say, the joke was lost on some.

Added to this mix would also be a smattering of interns from the Christian charity CARE. In a time of fear of outside lobbying and influence, I think it is good that charities such as this try to get more young people involved in the political process. I don't sign up to much of what CARE believes in or ascribes to, but it is important we have a healthy and diverse political process.

Over the years we had a few CARE interns in our office. There are two which I would particularly like to mention, though I am to a greater or lesser degree in touch with them all.

Firstly a young American guy called Travis. Just so you can picture him, he looks exactly like Timothy Claypole from the 1980s children's TV show *'Rentaghost'*. This was a cultural reference lost on Travis, a guy who had spent much of his childhood travelling countries in the Middle East with his missionary parents, rather than sat on a sofa in the Home Counties watching Dobbin the Pantomime Horse performing pratfalls for giggles.

Needless to say, this did not stop us endlessly referring to Travis as young Master Claypole, singing the theme to Rentaghost or saying things like *"Gadzooks!"*, *"Methinks"* or *"Mistress Meeker!"* for his entire year in Parliament. I expect nowadays they would call it workplace bullying.

Travis was also a bit of a ladies' man. Too cool for school. The sort of man who could look like an Elizabethan court jester and still carry it off. The sort of man who would turn up on Monday morning after a few hours snatched sleep and then tell you how he had randomly spent the weekend with pop star Daniel Bedingfield. He said he didn't know how he would make it to the end of the day, but I told him *"You've just gotta get through this"*. How we laughed.

At the same time we shared the office with a researcher called James who was working on issues concerning sport. Four grown men, if not mature men, sharing a tiny office space was always going to be a recipe for disaster, one way or another.

Dave would spend most Fridays away from the office in meetings. When he would phone up to ask me to get something off his computer that he urgently needed and had forgotten, I would always be only too happy to help – whilst at the same time changing the background on his computer screen from something celebrating Everton FC to a giant Watford FC logo or something equally inappropriate. This joke always got a double laugh, as I would forget that I had done this by the time Dave was back in the office on Monday and would surprise even myself with my comic genius.

I can remember odd renditions of songs such as *'Africa'* by Toto (trying to squeeze that line about the Serengeti in to fit the music, even though it's impossible to do); a well contested Parliamentary Fantasy Football competition (that continues to do this day), where Dr Dave won the initial title of winner of the Parliamentary Plate – and we duly awarded him a paper plate which we drew Big Ben on and his newly won title – which he received to the national anthem of Kazakhstan, as sung by Borat; as well as numerous texted phone messages to the office landline.

If you've never done it, sending a text message to a landline is absolutely fantastic and you must try it. I think one of us must have accidentally texted the wrong number once and then this little fad took hold. Clearly the phone companies do their best to pronounce words correctly and get the inflection correct, but quite often the robotic voice on the other end of the line would get it horribly wrong. I would often get texts I had sent to my colleagues from the Watford game on Saturday, sent back to the office landline for me to pick up on Monday. They should say things like: *"Watford goal. Mm. ☺ x"* What they would actually say is things like: *"Watford goal. Millimetre millimetre. Smiley face. Kiss."* There are literally seconds of entertainment to be had there.

Most of the banter was harmless, but then I do remember that Dr Dave once gaffer taped me to my chair for *'being annoying'*, so maybe not always so. He said in a court of law his actions would be legal as he had been a long-term sufferer from a medical condition known as *'Kerronic Irritation'*.

Travis eventually left, after his year was up, having survived being deported on numerous occasions – and he was replaced by a young Scottish girl called Linsay. We worried that this may seriously affect our football banter, but fortunately she was a big football fan (most of us didn't even know Motherwell had a professional team – and now having seen them play, I'm still not entirely convinced), though we were relieved to know our stereotypes were not entirely misplaced when we found out the car dealership next door to the ground was called *'Taggarts'*. I bet watching some of those matches must have been murder), and had a good sense of humour (and no access to gaffer tape).

It was around this time when the short-lived BBC political drama Party Animals came to our screens. Produced by the makers of the successful Channel 4 drama This Life, it told the fictionalised stories of those working in and around Parliament. The consultants on the show had apparently based some of the characters and events on real life occurrences, and pretty soon into the series it was picked up upon that one of the main characters bore a striking resemblance to me.

The series told stories of how many of the people in Parliament were heavy drinkers, taking drugs and having sex with most things that moved. Fortunately, or worryingly (depending on your perspective), my character didn't go in for any of that nonsense – he was the really boring, clean-living one, who was talking about the morality of politics and how it could be a force for good etc. If you have seen the series (and you can still get it on DVD), my character is the one played by Matt Smith, before his days in Doctor Who.

I was quite dismissive of similarities to begin with. Yes, he had been styled in the same way, with similar glasses, clothes and hairstyle, but that could just be coincidence. Then it turns out he is a Labour blogger, again it narrows the field but hardly conclusive. Then midway through the series, he starts trying to have a relationship with his intern. This was moderately embarrassing, because by this point I had just started a relationship with our intern (Linsay, not Travis).

It got to the point where every week we would watch what Danny Foster would get up to on Party Animals both intrigued and fearful of what storyline would be created next. Sadly the show was not recommissioned for a second series so we will never know the final outcome of the lives of these fictionalised versions of ourselves*, though we can take great solace/offence from knowing that our lives are too boring even for a BBC2 midweek audience to stomach. (*In real life, we got married – and are now going through a divorce. To my mind, Danny Foster escaped lightly.)

At the end of the first and final series, a few of the actors came into Parliament for a reception. All very lovely they were too. I spoke at length with Matt Smith and gave him a Transport and General Workers Union lanyard for his pass, which he was very taken with – or was too polite to say otherwise. He said: *"Oh you're me! That's good. You're the goodies, the other lot are the baddies!"* The politics of hope always wins through, even if it doesn't always get a second series.

Fortunately there was never much of a drinking culture in our office – unless large cups of subsidised tea and coffee count. There are several bars within Parliament which have been the ruin of many a political career. The MPs' bars of choice tend to be Annie's Bar (which for a time was turned into a makeshift pool hall), Members' Bar or Strangers' Bar. They are exclusive and salubrious but it doesn't mean there are not still punch ups and incidents which make the diary columns of some newspapers.

The choice for staff is much smaller. 1) Bellamy's Bar, next door to the café in 1 Parliament Street of the same name, was a haunt of choice for a time – though it has now been turned into a crèche. Sick, urine and crying faces everywhere – and then they turned it into a crèche; 2) Lords Bar is also a favourite, as you can get an evening meal to accompany your drink (or should it be the other way around). The only danger being that you might bump into a member of the House of Lords. This was a particular risk when I worked for a member of the House of Lords. One evening, drink in hand, I wandered over to peer (if you'll pardon the pun) at the annunciator screen to see if my employer was still in the Chamber or away for the evening. It was then I realised that he was quietly sitting under the annunciator eating his dinner. Ah well; 3) The Sports and Social, a few feet from the Lords Bar, well known for its pool table, darts board, karaoke nights and punch ups. That's unfair, it did get in the papers once when a Lord took a lady of the night there for an evening out. Euphemistically, I would say it had a *'lively'* atmosphere, like that bar Ben Kenobi takes Luke Skywalker into at the start of Star Wars – but I liked its spirit and charm. Karaoke nights though were a time when all bets were off – a time when one too many would have one too many and then melees would usually ensue. Don't get me wrong, some of the worst offenders were MPs who loved the atmosphere, as well as doing a turn on the mic. Those were the sort of evenings that most would flock to the Sports and Social, and the rest of us would pack up and head for home.

See I am the political equivalent of Ovaltine.
To Matt Smith, I can only apologise so much.

4. Local Government

In the same way that London is not necessarily the centre of the UK, it should be remembered that Parliament is not necessarily the heart of UK democracy and politics. We have a devolved system of power at the local level, where councils and local authorities up and down the land can contribute greatly to the wellbeing of national life.

Did that sound convincing?

Whilst undoubtedly local politics can make a massive difference to the lives of local people on a micro scale, very few people would see the life of a local councillor as having the same allure and appeal as that of an MP. It's hardly glamorous. I speak as someone who has served at various levels in local government over the years.

I began at our local parish council, the lowest rung of the political ladder. For those of you who now have an image of those parish council meetings from The Vicar of Dibley, you have it just about right – although our real-life meetings were far less professional and far less believable than those recreated in that TV comedy.

I had been asked to stand for the parish council because of the work I had been doing in our local community outside of politics. I was doing youth work at one of our local churches and had led a number of social action projects with them. For example, we cleaned graffiti off the slides and swings at the local park; we identified and measured pot holes in the roads; we collected litter; we set up a recycling project and much more besides. To me, those are the sort of things you do if you want a happy, healthy and cohesive society – small things to contribute to the common good. For others, it's what you force yourself to do if you want to get elected.

A by-election had arisen in our village. I hadn't been very involved in local politics, and hadn't been particularly interested. The chances of Labour sweeping to victory in the sweet Hertfordshire commuter villages, such as the one I grew up in, are unlikely at the best of times – but I had been told that the Parish Council needed fresh blood and, as someone who was prepared to put the work in, I should give it a go.

I had been told that parish council elections in this particular area were traditionally non-party political. Sure there were Conservative, Lib Dem and Labour members on the council but, since its inception, the tradition was that party politics was kept out of it and people would stand as independents on their own merits. I was also told that quite often they couldn't even find people to fill the spaces on the parish council, so if I put my name up I may be fortunate enough to be co-opted unopposed.

So that is the long and short of how I ended up in a fairly acrimonious head to head battle at the ballot box with the former Lib Dem Chair of the Parish Council.

I was blissfully unaware that the Lib Dem machine locally had taken a decision to try and take over the Parish Council and would now label all its candidates accordingly – pointing the finger at everyone else as being untrustworthy for not openly declaring their politics.

To be honest, when I did find out, I wasn't that fussed. It wasn't like I desperately wanted to be a parish councillor, and I suspected that if this guy had chaired the whole thing previously, he would not only be a shoo-in but also incredibly capable too. But, ironically, it turned out that this decision to openly label as being Lib Dem backfired and I was elected by more than a two to one majority – probably by little old Tory ladies with blue rinses, eager to keep the Lib Dems out.

That was my introduction to local politics. Latterly I spoke to the MP I was working for, to see if this experience was uncommon. He said that his first elected role in politics was on his local parish council – staunchly Conservative, with no Labour (or Lib Dem) representatives. He had been asked to stand through the work he had been doing at his church (predominantly work with Fairtrade projects, if I remember correctly) and had thought it pretty pointless given the likely electoral outcome. Where he was standing for election the parish council had decided that people would openly stand on party political tickets – so chances of an upset were remote. It turns out though that the

Conservative candidates failed to submit valid forms to the local authority – their applications to stand were subsequently ruled invalid, and he and his friend were elected in their place for a four year term.

It always strikes me slightly bizarre when parish councils attempt to be party political and partisan. You will be discussing issues such as dog poo bins, the condition of bus shelters or footpaths, or maintaining a couple of patches of grass not maintained by the local authority – it's hard to find a party political approach to such matters. There's a small budget and great opportunities that people will waste it on various schemes and appeals that are unlikely to succeed – in a larger authority, teams of trained officials (specialists in their own field), will give expert advice on every issue. They particularly will tell you the liability for decisions, projects and appeals you may wish to undertake. In a parish council, this is all left up to one unelected official (the Clerk) and the elected members, who often will have little experience of the legal or council processes that are being jumped into with both feet.

Don't get me wrong, I admire the contribution that parish councils try to make to our local and national life – it's just that, from my own experience, I think we could do without them. Given the costs and the amount that can go horribly wrong, it would be far better off to transfer these powers back to local authorities which are better regulated and more professional in their work.

If the parish council membership is a bit eccentric, the types that get involved in standing for local government are even more bizarre. In the tier above parish councils, depending on the structure of your authority, you will either have a district council (overseeing matters such as recycling, planning, litter collection, leisure, housing etc) and a county council (overseeing matters such as education, the police* and highways) – or you will have a unitary authority that oversees the equivalent work of both the district and county council. (*Although probably not now you have a Police and Crime Commissioner.) Confused? You should be.

The reason that there is such a weird mix of members on most local authorities is because there is genuine power in these structures – and most parties will be unable to find around 50 candidates to stand who are both capable and sane, as well as willing to put in the work required to become elected. Local politics is a lot of leafleting, a lot of knocking on doors and a lot of going to meetings, sometimes at the council, sometimes in the local community.

All human life is here on your local authority: The truly committed; those that should be committed (to an institution); massive egos; the busybodies and, last of all, those who want to become MPs.

I am always reassured that those who have thought putting down four years as a local councillor on your CV – to seem that they are a serious hardworking individual committed both to their party and to the local community – will have to spend endless nights being frustrated by people who couldn't give the first toss about Government or any future career ambitions.

Discussions and contributions that go on for hours. Perpetually discussing the same points over and over. The press has gone home at 10pm and there are no member of the public present, yet still Cllr Joe Bloggs wants to make the same point he has made 313 times before about how under a different administration he used to get given black rubbish bags by the council for his rubbish, but now he doesn't, and clearly this will increase fly-tipping as a result. You get the idea.

There should be a function in place so that when someone says: *"I agree wholeheartedly with the points that have been made previously"*, that if they do not then immediately sit down and instead subject the room to 10 minutes of exactly the same points their party leader gave them to recite on a piece of A4 at the start of the evening, that we should be able to ask the Chair to press a big red button that drops the speaker through a trap door and into a swimming pool underneath. (Sadly, this will never happen though due to a combination of health and safety concerns and constraints to capital budgets.)

A lot of nonsense is spoken about the amount that our local representatives are paid. Parish councillors don't get any expenses (probably rightly so, especially if it's performance related pay) and those on local authorities are hardly generously reimbursed.

The authority I was on was one of the lowest paid in the entire country. Having had a couple of years as a parish councillor, I was used to not getting paid to work myself into the ground for the local community, so it wasn't a big thing – but the amount of conversations with people who insinuated councillors only took on the role for the money and big kickbacks, was astounding.

When I was first elected onto my local district council, we were paid around £3,000 a year. When you compare this against the hours I worked on behalf of local people – whether that was in the Council Chamber, out in the local community holding advice surgeries and attending meetings or undertaking casework – I would not even have been earning the Minimum Wage. I would have been financially better off chucking it all in and going to work at McDonalds.

Councillors' pay rarely increases. In difficult economic times, there are always better things to invest the money in – but even in good economic times, it is a hard sell to take the recommendations of the independent advisory board who suggest councillors should be paid at a higher level. Why should people be paid adequately for their work? They should be pleased to do it for nothing. If you let councillors have the final vote on their own pay levels, they will rarely, if ever, push for pay increases – even when an outside body specifically recommends this – because they know it will be unpopular with the voters and an opportunity for colleagues from other parties to make political capital from this. So what you end up with is an underpaid and undervalued role that only those rich enough to absorb the cost can undertake.

The only way I could make being a councillor work was by balancing it with a full-time job. I worked in Parliament during the day, then I came home and picked up all my casework and went out to my meetings. Most evenings there would be a handful of calls on my answerphone, usually complaining about the dire housing situation. Many of these would berate me for not picking up the phone, either because I didn't want to talk to the general public or I was doing something far more exciting with the proceeds of my generous expenses. It hadn't occurred to them that whilst it demanded hours of my daily life to sort their problems (which I was only too happy to do), being a councillor is not a full-time job in the paid sense of that phrase.

I would spend most of my evenings and weekends going to meetings where genuinely frustrated people would tell me how I didn't really care about them and wouldn't help anyway. Which was rather ironic given that if I didn't really care, I wouldn't have turned up in the first place to get moaned at. For the most part, I let it wash over me and got on with the job of serving my local community.

Actually, that's not strictly true, as outlined before, with the exception of a ginormous blunder on the declaration of candidates forms, it was unlikely I would ever represent my local village. I did give it a go and got within 200 votes of beating the incumbent, but in my heart I knew that was not to be. I ended up being asked to stand in another by-election for the same District Council in a neighbouring community.

I loved South Oxhey, still do. Very down-to-earth place where people always have time to chat to you. This old GLC estate had rather bizarrely been dropped onto the outskirts of Watford, bringing with it many many salt-of-the-earth, old-school East End cockneys in the 1950s and 1960s. I liked it also because unlike most political campaigns, people would not simply be polite to your face to get rid of you – if these people had a problem, they would tell you to your face. You knew where you stood and there was no façade. I liked that a lot.

On the day of the by-election I was out knocking on doors, trying to persuade people to vote. A little old lady came up to me telling me how I'd be exactly the same as all the others, and there was no point in voting, and that no-one stood up for the poor and vulnerable anymore, and local services were going downhill. I thanked her for her time and honesty, and wished her well as I turned to walk away. She said: *"Well, you better do a good job when you're elected. I've already voted for you by postal!"*

Local politics can be a nasty business. Perhaps it's to do with the egos or the sense of power, but local election campaigns do not need much encouragement to turn nasty.

Leaflets full of misinformation and false stats. Claims and counter claims. Nasty personal venal attacks. There is little regulation on what can and cannot be said and some parties and individuals take full advantage.

Just this week I saw a local election leaflet for a political party, I won't name them here but I am sure you can guess, whose entire leaflet was either disingenuous or full of incorrect information – with the sole intention of getting elected. Dodgy bar charts that bear no relation to actual statistics, attacks on the local councillors, followed by a claim that Party A cannot win here – only Party C can beat Party B here. A quick check on the electoral stats for this seat when I got home indicated that contrary to what this leaflet said Party A (who could not win here) had 2 of the current councillors, Party B had one councillor and Party C had 0 councillors having finished a distant third.

In local politics this sort of behaviour is par for the course but it does not make it right or proper. What it does is to encourage others to enter into similar underhand tactics as they believe they need to retaliate. Party C then says that everyone else is behaving poorly and only they can bring back proper values at the ballot box. Etc. A self-fulfilling prophecy that sends us on an inevitable downward spiral.

These leaflets and door-to-door campaigns work on the principle that most people do not know what is going on with their local council and who their local councillors are. Sadly this is a fair assumption to make in most cases. Therefore you can say whatever you like (if you have no scruples) and then when someone contradicts you say: *"They would say that, wouldn't they?"*

The problem with negative campaigning is that it works. I always tried to counter this by working hard in the local community, putting out leaflets that tried to inform people what was actually going on (with as little spin as possible), but there are times when your opponents will win by not playing fair. As a Christian in politics, your choice is how do you react to this. Do you rise above it or try to get even. If you pick the latter option, the bitterness will consume you and destroy you.

Politics is a dirty game, but there is no better feeling than winning fairly.

Whenever we used to have conversations about how unfair our electoral system is, or that it simply isn't fair when people don't play according to the rules, and that everything is unjust, Dr Dave would normally chip in: *"At least they can't make you pregnant."*

A great piece of political insight for all men setting out on a political career, there – though not particularly helpful for any women in politics.

Local politics can be as much about luck as it is judgement. Being in the right place at the right time is a skill you can't teach. I was happy being a simple local councillor. For five years I held the Housing and Environment brief, partly this was because I had a passion for helping those going through tough times and that were in need of support – partly it was because no-one else wanted the job.

Put simply, we do not have enough affordable or social housing in the South East. People who already have housing are not that interested in seeing new housing being built because it puts greater strain on local services and obscures their view. You would have thought that politicians would have a duty and responsibility to say that we need to build more housing – and help find sustainable ways to do this, which work well with existing homes. What actually happens is that most politicians go into panic mode and resort to their default knee-jerk setting of opposing all new homes anywhere. Not in my back yard – and hang the consequences. As soon as that becomes the predominant position, all you are doing is dealing with the fall-out and managing an escalating series of problems.

My favourite sort of NIMBY is the short-termist, nothing happened before I turned up, but I want things to stay exactly how they are now. Let me give you an example: When I was a parish councillor, I was approached by families complaining that some new houses were going to be built near them. It was not an unreasonable concern to have. Yes, the houses were in the Local Plan, but it was right that any development was in-keeping with the local area and not detrimental for local families nearby. It was then that you looked at the detail of the complaints. They were unhappy that the proposed houses were to be built on an old school playing field.

The Government had shut this school (and many others) in the late 1980s and early 1990s, and this was the latest attempt to build houses on the old site. What some of these families had failed to recognise was that the very houses they now lived in had also been built on the old school site and playing fields. Not a matter of principle then against losing school fields and green areas per se, no, you got your house on the playing field and now want to stop anyone else doing the same. Ironically, the schools had been shut due to falling school roles (i.e. a lack of children in the surrounding area making a local school viable), as soon as all the houses were built and several families moved in, they had the opposite problem – large numbers of children but no local school to place them in. It's almost as if some decisions are not properly and strategically thought through, isn't it?

I had been asked to consider going on a leadership training course for gifted young councillors. As always *'young'* is relative, I had been a parish councillor at 23 and then up onto the district council at 24, I was still learning the ropes. My then group leader opposed me going on the course because she thought I would try and take her job. Ironically, she lost her seat at the elections and I was asked to take her job anyway, but without the training. I had no ambitions, but these things have a funny way of working their way out.

Anything shy of 50 is young in council terms though. The only place I am still considered *'young'* is at council meetings or at church. It's an odd pairing.

I was a local councillor, in one form or another, from early 2001 through to late 2009.I only turned it in when I was offered a job working for the church on poverty issues and working with the media for an Archbishop (as you do), and it was too good an opportunity to turn down. Also it was on the other side of the country. My colleagues, and residents, asked me to stay but my mind was made up.

I had a good time in local politics, you really could help people in a practical everyday way. But it doesn't pay the bills. Maybe I'll go back to it one day.

5. Running For Parliament – Getting Selected

If you have spent any amount of time working in and around politics – whether that's in local government, working in parliament, knocking on doors for someone you barely like, or through your involvement in some grassroots community group – inevitably, at some point, the thought of standing for Parliament yourself will cross your mind.

It may have something to do with ambition or ego, or the pretence of wanting to serve your constituents, but more often than not it is due to the overwhelming fact that anyone could do this job better than the current MPs we have. That may sound incredibly dismissive of the majority of MPs who are probably trying to make a good fist of a difficult job, and I am sure many of them do contribute a great deal for the betterment of their communities, but at the same time some of them shouldn't be allowed out of their own house.

The vast majority of representatives come from the political classes. For all the talk of open selection processes, regardless of the party concerned, see how many Parliamentarians are from the affluent middle classes. See how many have a background working behind the scenes for the main players in Westminster. See how many went to Oxbridge. See how many are white men. See how many previously had careers as solicitors or barristers. For the most part this is a closed club, and people like you and me are not invited.

Now, before I write a chapter about parliamentary selections, I should make a couple of things clear:

1) I write this out of my own experiences as someone who has sought to stand as a parliamentary candidate.* So I might be biased. (*Have you ever noticed how close the word *'parliamentary'* looks to the word *'paramilitary'*? Before you continue reading this section, please check you have the right one in your head. Thanks.)

2) I fully understand that by writing anything about the internal selection processes of a political party that I have completely undermined any small hope I may have had of ever getting selected again. The upper

echelons of the political classes are not known for their sense of humour or love of satire (unless it's Gilbert and Sullivan). I am willing to take that risk – frankly moving my selection status from *'unlikely'* to *'never going to happen'* to *'blacklisted for being an embarrassing troublemaker'* is going to make little difference to my career prospects in the future. However these are my views and my views alone, not those of any friends, family or peripheral others who may now be sullied into the bargain for my frankness.

Let's get it right from the outset, getting elected to Parliament *is* a career. This is where real power and status resides and every effort will be taken to keep the hoi polloi out. (If you do not know what the phrase *'hoi polloi'* means, this means people like you.)

Parliament is deliberately set up to look and run like a gentleman's club or public school. Obviously when I say *'gentleman's club'*, I mean in the sense of the Carlton Club or Liberal Club, where men smoking cigars and drinking tumblers of fine malt whisky are waited on by a butler, as a fine array of hunting trophies look onwards and outwards from the walls. I do not mean *'gentleman's club'* in the sense of Stringfellowes or Spearmint Rhino. Then again I have not been to either sort of establishment – and I am unlikely to – so it may be this view comes from some sort of deep-seated reverse-snobbery, or secret jealousy, I have hidden deep within myself.

Parliament is meant to be intimidating and overwhelming for those who have not been brought up in such luxurious surroundings – and it is meant to be reassuring and familiar for those whose backgrounds on the playing fields of Eton have had it repeatedly drummed into them that they were born to lead.

Through the course of my job and various political appointments, I have had the great pleasure and privilege to visit a great number of schools and youth groups to talk to young people about politics and the importance of civic engagement. I am always struck by the different answers when you ask the question: *"What would you like to be when you grow up?"*

Nowadays I am saddened to hear most boys reply to this question with things like *'footballer'* or *'actor'* and girls say things like *'model'*, *'singer'* or even *'WAG'*. That is a sign of our celebrity driven culture, where people and careers are disposable for 15 seconds of what can loosely be described as *'fame'*. But let's put that great number of answers to one side for the time being and focus on those that give more considered answers.

In your local state school, you will generally hear boys saying *"I would like to be a [policeman/soldier/mechanic/fireman]"* and girls saying *"I would like to be a [teacher/nurse]"*. I could write endless chapters on what that says about the ingrained bias society assigns to certain gender defined roles – in other words that popular culture and media tells young men that they should be hands-on manual workers and that young women should be carers, educators or somehow secondary to the aspirations of men. Equally I could argue that it shows boys and girls are simply different with different outlooks, desires and skills. I am sure either argument could land me in potential hot water – and, to be honest, it's not the point I am trying to make here.

Ask someone at a public school what they would like to be when they grow up and the answer tends to be tangibly different: *"I am going to be a [barrister/diplomat/doctor]"*. The doubt has been removed. They know what they want to be – usually a high status professional role – and they are going to be it once they have got their grades.

Perhaps it is the level of schooling, perhaps it is the ingrained sense of entitlement, perhaps it is the old school networks of special handshakes and knowing winks that means these people get on. I think it is more likely to do with the great wedges of cash that these individuals (or rather their parents) have that allows them better opportunities in life than many of their contemporaries.

There is little that can be done to tackle such societal unfairness. Money talks. All we can do is ensure that every child has the best education possible at their local school and that they are consistently told that they are special and important – and that they have an important role to play in society and the democratic process.

The other thing we could do is make our political processes more open and democratic. But that's unlikely to ever happen.

In most political parties, the first step (following someone discerning themselves that they may like to run for parliament) is that an initial vetting process is undertaken.

I am taking it as read that if you want to run for Parliament you are looking to do so via one of the main political parties, and have not only already decided which one you would most like to represent but also become an active member within that party.

Too many people, normally those who want to *'do politics'* (as if it is a gap year from their work at the local legal practice), seem to have a road to Damascus experience where God tells them to become an MP or Prime Minister and are then astounded that they should have already picked which political party to support.

Our political system is rarely personality led. We have government by parliament, by democratic majority – rather than a presidential system where one individual calls all the shots and carries voters from all sides through sheer cult of personality. If you want to see a government like that then I would point you towards the American political model. We tend to do things differently.

OK, you could argue that there are rare exceptions. Possibly Winston Churchill could have had the full support of the British people and parliament for his stoic resistance to the Nazis during the Second World War – but then again he did lose to Clement Atlee's domestic reform agenda directly after the conflict, so that probably doesn't stack up so well.

Possibly Margaret Thatcher, with her divide and conquer mentality that ensured she took great swathes of the working classes and the popular vote across three General Elections – despite being hated passionately by significant swathes outside the South East and in certain industries – but could she have been anything other than a *'True Blue'* Conservative? I couldn't see her defecting when those around her got out the knives – she made her political bed and had to lie in it.

Or possibly even Tony Blair. He took Labour into the political centre-ground and delivered three General Election wins by abandoning a great deal of the established Labour ideology and rhetoric. His dad was a Conservative, and you could see him having stood for any of the major parties – arguably Labour was just the vehicle that allowed him into Government to deliver his own agenda. It's the most plausible example from modern times, but I think it is slightly harsh on Blair who would probably argue that he was always Labour, with a clear fairness and social justice agenda, just in a different style to what had gone before, bringing his party into a modern existence. In America you have well-known individuals being headhunted and wooed in a professional sense by both main parties simply because their name, brand and reputation can play well at the ballot box.

Once you've identified the party you would like to represent and submitted an initial CV (in standard format, across four pages of A4 – no-one wants to hear about your summer job at Greggs following your A-Levels). If you survive that first sift, and 99% of people will, you are then invited to a panel interview.

These interviews tend to take place in your region of choice. You may choose any number of regions that you wish to stand in, but generally speaking this interview will be the region you live in. For me, living just outside Watford, you might have expected a trip into London for this 30 minute assessment – but instead I found myself taking a series of trains (firstly into London and then another back out again) to reach an interview in Ipswich.

Whoever designed the regions – the ones we use for European elections – needs a seriously good talking to. Down in Cornwall and Devon, you are in the same region as the Scilly Isles and Gibraltar – that must be a beggar for canvassing.

Ipswich is fine and that, don't get me wrong – even when on the day in question they were clearly taking boat-fulls of rotting rubbish out of the docks – it's just not somewhere I have a great affinity with.

I arrived 10 minutes early for the interview, as is my general habit with any interview for anything, and the whole thing was over within

10 minutes. In fact I think I had answered the vast majority of their questions with my first answer. Generally questions will be: *"Why do you want to be an MP"*, *"Why would you be a good MP"*, *"Have you done any campaigning/canvassing/stood for office before"*, a random question about something topical (mine was about keeping the pound, I think, which is an interestingly divisive topic for any occasion, let alone an interview for being a prospective MP!) and the standard one about the whipping.

Before you become too concerned about exactly what that final question may entail, it is a fairly bog-standard predictable question about collective democracy, rather than one about what you get up to behind closed doors with consenting adults. It might be an obvious question, but it is one that catches a lot of people out. It is phrased in a fairly open way asking if you would ever vote against your party in Parliament (there is an identical question for would be councillors, you simply replace the word *'Parliament'* for *'the Council chamber'*). A one word answer is not sufficient. This is a rigorous test, not a tick box.

The panel is made up of around 4 people. At least one of these will be a regional official, one typically will be a National Executive Member and at least one is likely to be a former candidate – then it's perm any one from three for your final interrogator. Each of them knows what this question is all about. It is essentially saying are you: *"an ego/a nutter/a general liability to what the party wants to achieve"*, however it is couched in such a way that the unsuspecting amateur might jump in with both feet. *"Let me give you an example"* one of the panel will say helpfully, *"cuts need to be made to your local school/hospital because there is no money for improvements, and your constituents are not happy with this, whose side will you take"*.

It's a deliberately loaded and unlikely scenario. It is begging you to say *"I will stand up for my constituents at all costs, I will say 'NO, Whitehall, you have gone too far this time', and call an emergency debate in the Commons."* Such a response will inevitably invalidate your application. If you want to be extra safe, go with the Gordon Gekko line that the party is always right and knows better than you. Otherwise sit on a fence and say that every avenue must be investigated, but you are sure such a standoff would never be allowed to happen – that you would represent your constituents but, ultimately, that collective responsibility must be respected. If you have to balance budgets and get votes through, sometimes bad things will happen in your area – the challenge is to ensure that is prevented before a key vote occurs.

"OK, OK," sighs a weary interviewer who has heard this pragmatic fence-sitting response from 3 aspiring candidates already today, *"but is there any reason you can think of where you would not vote with your party?"* Again you can straight-bat your response and say that the party is always 100% right, never getting any major decision wrong on anything ever (they like that response a lot), however you might like to be honest and say only if it was a clear matter of ethical/religious conscience. *"Such as what"* will be the response, their ears now pricked for the calamitous balls-up you are one breath away from making. Do NOT say anything clever like suggesting an unlikely situation where the Government decides to go to war on a false premise, without the clear moral authority and endorsement of the United

Nations. That way danger lies. Instead consider waffling about your clear moral and ethical traditions, sticking up for constituents/public services and the rights of man, no matter where they are – or better still, just say you can't think of any at this moment in time and such a situation would be very very unlikely to ever occur, and if it did you'd talk to the Whips first and they would probably be very understanding and tell you not to come to the vote that day. Essentially, the Whips are your masters and you must remember this (and you must recite this publicly like a mantra before you are allowed in the game).

That's clearly only the approach of the one party I'm familiar with, but I expect the general experience will be the same whichever way you lean politically.

I also went for an interview for the Co-operative Party Panel. This was much tougher and more rigorous – and enjoyable – than the previous interview. The Co-operative Party are a sister party of the Labour Party and they have an electoral agreement where members of both institutions can stand on a joint ticket (though never against each other).

That process began with a written request, then a CV and then finally an intensive day of interviews involving a written test and an oral presentation.

It felt like you were being asked proper questions about why you were involved in politics, rather than simply ticking boxes on someone's elimination sheet. Getting that certificate saying I was now on the Co-op Party Panel, signed by the National Secretary of the Party (actually signed by them rather than an electronic signature), was one of the proudest moments of my life. In those days it was generally hard to get on that panel of candidates – as the above process might suggest.

On my interview day, in London, I was locked in the basement of a hotel in London Bridge with another aspiring candidate. She was bright, brilliant and, frankly, much more likely to be an MP than I ever was – she was a member of the Greater London Assembly at the time and sure enough, subsequently, she would become a fine MP. We were both tasked with writing an Early Day Motion based on the Co-operative Party's Manifesto for Local Government (don't pretend you haven't read it!) and once we had done this, the next part was to give an oral presentation justifying your choice.

We both reflected for a few seconds and then burst into a productive whizz of creative fervour. At the end of 10 minutes, I had a perfectly formed three line EDM (one complete sentence, broken into three parts by cleverly placed semi-colons). My colleague had nigh on 5 pages of incisive, well-researched political reflections which may, on a good day, transform our world for the better. You can now probably see why she is now an MP and I am not.

It used to be that you stayed on your party's Parliamentary Panel for life – unless you did something very silly – but the Co-op Party apparently only keeps the panel for the life of one election and you have to reapply. Having gone through the process around 10 years ago now, I am not sure I have the energy and patience to go through that sort of intensive grilling again for one election in which I am not likely to get a winnable seat anyway.

Once you are on a panel – and that is easier said than done in some cases, for example trade unions run their own Parliamentary Panels to feed into the Labour Party process but in ten years of attempting to get on to it I have always been told that it is shut to new applicants. Clearly that is not the case as there have been two or three General Elections in that time, you just get the impression certain people (outsiders) are not welcome – then you have the challenge of finding a seat.

You would think that the natural choice would be to stand in the seat where you live. However there are problems with this. The vast majority of seats will not change hands at a General Election – not unless it is a landslide year like 1983 or 1997. Most seats will be of one political hue and are likely to stay so for the lifetime of their existence. This either means that: 1) you are likely to be in a seat which is deemed safe for an opposing party and you have little or no chance of winning it 2) you are likely to be in a seat which is deemed safe for your party which means there are a long line of people already lined up to take it over when there is a vacancy.

Usually this probably is eased slightly by the fact that there will hopefully be a number of seats for your party of choice in your region. For example, if you are a Conservative living in deepest darkest Surrey, there should be opportunities around the corner, if not on your doorstep – same goes for Labour supporters living in Greater Manchester. Your real problem occurs if you are a Conservative living in Scotland or a Labour supporter living in the Home Counties – your chances for a winnable seat are very very slim.

As someone who fits into that latter category, I know this problem only too well – but even in the South East of England there are a handful of swing seats that could turn red in a good year. You've always got a shot, right? You'd like to think so, but what actually happens is that before you even get near an election the seats have been carved up. You know it's going to be an even worse situation in the safe seats in an area you don't live, but if you can fluke the selection through hard work and charm you are sitting pretty. Your final option is to target key marginal seats in different regions (which you hopefully have some affinity to) and hope that they are so marginal other people – and the party – won't be bothered enough to rig it properly.

I've had a go at all of the above, with limited success. The odds are not in your favour, no matter how good you may be.

Of course, there are things that can improve your chances of success:

1)   Have friends in high places. In some selections, you will be phoning members and knocking on doors, asking for support – and one or more of your opponents will have high ranking Cabinet Ministers doing this on their behalf. Given the choice between some spotty oik chancing his arm on your doorstep and the recommendation of some guys you've seen on telly, it's not a difficult choice to make.

2)   Be on the inside track. In other words, be the preferred candidate. Of course, this then begs the question of how you become the preferred candidate. We might like to pretend that selection processes are fair, open and totally outside the political will of others, but we know that not to be the case from hard fought experience. It used to be the case that

you were not allowed to do any canvassing for support before the selection process had been formally opened – anyone contacting members before the process was underway would be eliminated. However, in reality, certain candidates would miraculously find an up to date membership list and be able to go and talk to members personally ahead of a declaration. The party rarely if ever took action against such lapses, and that was unsurprising given where the information generally leaked from. Essentially you need to be in on the stitch up if you are to profit from it. Who has an interest in the outcome of selection (aside from the candidates)? The Party, trade unions, local constituency members. Hopefully they all want a process to go a certain way, otherwise you have three preferred candidates fighting it out to the death. All local constituency branches get a nomination, as will several trade union affiliate branches (however they are unlikely to give you their support, unless you are one of their official candidates). There is then a shortlisting process where the constituency's executive committee decide who goes through to a final hustings – you would think that anyone with a nomination would get through, but actually this is the final stage where a potential winner can get ruled out by a local faction who does not want their name in the frame because they have a chance of winning. Finally you have the final hustings – and we'll get to that later.

3) Be a woman. Whenever I bring up the issue of All Women Shortlists, I inevitably get accused of being anti-women and a misogynist with a vested interest. The truth is nothing of the sort – although I cannot deny I have a penis and this clearly undermines anything further I say on the matter. I want to see a political system where women are an active and central part of the democratic process at all levels – I do not just want to see a handful of middle class women being given a leg up over local candidates. I want to see a system where women are not seen or treated as a minority group or a weaker sex that needs to be fast-tracked. I want to see strong female representatives that are there on their own merits, working hard on behalf of local people who they genuinely care about. I want to not only see women MPs but also more women councillors, more women Constituency Chairs and more women Constituency Secretaries. Do you genuinely think AWS does that? Does it tackle the

inherent problems we have in the structures of our political parties, or is it simply window dressing, massaging the figures at the top end to hide the systemic problems that will forever remain? I have campaigned on behalf of many very good, very capable, very strong women – mostly on Open Shortlists. Most of the women I know want to be judged on their skills and abilities, rather than on whether they have a vagina or not. What we have created is a system where a certain type of woman, a political class, can go around the country trying to get selected in several seats – we have not encouraged local working class women to represent their own communities.

From my experience you have a handful of women turning up at every AWS selection, going from constituency to constituency seeking nominations. Most are professional women (mainly from the legal profession, interestingly) or former MPs, or those that have worked within Parliament, who can devote enough time and money to perpetually traipse around the country, rather than those that go out and earn an living or have to juggle everyday affairs into the bargain. There are exceptions to this rule, but that is a fair generalisation. I don't want to personalise this debate, but there is one leading former Cabinet Minister who constantly talks about how we need more AWS selections everywhere, and then supported her husband to win a seat which should nominally have been AWS. It is about power and pulling up the ladders to stop others following the course you have set out. The same person also contested a deputy leadership contest in her political party saying that people should vote for her because she was a woman (not because of the skills or insight she brought to the role) and that men had been *'doing this thing for too long'* – seemingly oblivious to the fact that one of her opponents was also a woman. It's bizarre and not helpful to furthering genuine equality and fairness into our structures and wider society.

4) Move to the constituency. Clearly being local to the seat helps. You can befriend all the members and the local powerbrokers (if not the national ones). I know several people who have done this – again they had the independent means to do so, not all of us can up sticks, leave our jobs, to move to an entirely new part of the country a few months

before a possible selection process. Maybe you could take a decent guess at which seats might be coming up on the horizon. This cheers me up greatly when I think about the amount of political operators over the last 20 years or so who have relocated to places like Bolsover or Bootle in the hope of clinching a contest that never arises. This is a great way to lose the best years of your life. Even if you call it right and an ageing politician decides they will step down, there is nothing to stop the party making the seat AWS or parachuting in a different candidate (or both).

Really the question is not how capable you are, but rather how much do you want to win. How much do you want to put on the line? How much can you afford to lose?

We have a more professionalised political system than ever before, that means there is less and less opportunity for those outside the political bubble to gate-crash the party. We pretend that is not the case, but it was ever thus.

Also the high number of children of MPs who become Parliamentary candidates in winnable seats – and who subsequently become MPs – do we think this is because they have inherited a political gene or because the political dynasty knows who helps pull the strings? Regardless of party it happens time and again. Time and again.

I spoke to someone inside the inner sanctum of one of the political party HQs once about my own chances of a marginal/semi-winnable seat at a forthcoming election, as someone who had sweated blood for the party on the doorstep and in local government. I was told that Parliament was not for people like me – some people are there to do the donkey work for others. We do the heavy lifting to allow the Special Advisors and favoured sons (and it is usually sons – it is far more interesting to look at safe Parliamentary seats that do NOT go AWS, than those that do, to see who might have been earmarked for that seat) to get a free run at it. Local councillor is the political equivalent of saying *'Worked at Pizza Hut'* when it comes to CV credibility. I was told my best chance was to aim at a particular seat (which I won't name) where Labour was in third place and then in a couple of elections time, we might come through the middle and win. The thing is the person I was talking to was being deadly serious. The best chance for someone outside the main game in Westminster is to pick somewhere relatively unwinnable, where the other parties are ahead of you, and then in 10 years' time a combination of your hard work and the ineptitude of the other two main parties may allow you one term in Parliament (and that is if the Party doesn't see this coming and drop someone else into this opportunity you have created). And that is the BEST chance? I am sorry, but life is too short and special to be used as cannon-fodder in this way – much better to focus on local politics where you can make a real difference in people's lives on a daily basis without much external intervention.

I spoke to another leading individual – without giving too much away, let us say they are a major powerbroker behind the scenes – who said that someone like me may get a by-election *'soon'* because of the credibility of being a hardworking, reliable local councillor who had practical experience of working with national government. That was around 6 or 7 years ago and I am still waiting. In fact I put my name in for a Parliamentary by-election down the road, a while back – didn't even get shortlisted, but then again neither did most of the local councillors in that seat who put in for it, and neither did the preferred local candidate (another leading councillor), so it could have been worse. You can't take it personally. In that case, from a field of hundreds, two women from outside the constituency were the only ones shortlisted because the party wanted *'a fresh start'*.

All parties do it, but the engineering to stop certain candidates getting in is frightening. I don't honestly think I've ever been a victim of that, I just don't think I am important enough to have ever been noticed! All rules go out of the window for by-elections – people submit their names, a long-list is drawn up, then a shortlist decided upon by the national party. It will tend to look like this: Preferred candidate, a woman who is not local and not likely to win, a BAME (Black and Minority Ethnic – their description, not mine) candidate who is not local and not likely to win and then A.N.Other but also unlikely to win (maybe a young candidate who needs encouragement and a bit of profile built). This list is then put to the constituency party who then joins the dots to give the candidate we all wanted in the first place.

Apparently it's slightly different in the Conservative Party where they do not really go in for canvassing and door-knocking for selections. It's a one day interview, meet the members over a glass of something bubbly, a quick mini hustings and then a vote. All very civilised.

I don't know Lib Dem selections for a fact, but given that our local Lib Dems have just invited people to stand for them at a Council level without any experience or even fondness of the Lib Dems, I wouldn't be surprised if you didn't necessarily have to be a member to stand.

I lose count of how many Parliamentary Selection contests I have been involved in as a candidate, such is my success, but I think it's nearing double figures already over two elections. I've not bothered myself with losing any this time around yet, but maybe I will in an attempt to prove myself wrong.

I've had some truly wonderfully bizarre experiences, most of them in Scottish selections. I was at one particularly entertaining selection where I realised, latterly, I had been shortlisted for the final hustings in order to make up the numbers – the powerbrokers locally astutely recognising I had no chance of winning – where I was beaten by someone who turned up half an hour late because they couldn't find the venue.

Another I was told to go home to my own country, by someone who was born overseas. At the same selection people chatted throughout my address to the meeting and took phone calls, saying things like *"No, he's rubbish, he'll be finished soon"* and other such character building phrases.

I lived patches of my life in Scotland and at the time was married to a Scot who had assured me that I would be OK (i.e. not lynched) so long as I didn't speak. So I only have myself to blame with those instances.

On another occasion I had an opponent pull out their birth certificate to prove that, although they had never lived in the seat at any point, around 35 years ago they had been born at the local hospital. This still made them more local than me and won them the selection. How do you compete with such determination to win?

I've even been at selections where there have been more candidates than local party members.

Maybe losing, and the inevitability of losing has made me feel a bit jaded? Don't let me put you off. I'll be here to offer you a shoulder to cry on when you need it later.

Having said that, I have won one Parliamentary selection once. And it was my home seat. Can you guess how it turned out?

6. Running For Parliament – The General Election

If you are lucky enough to win a selection contest, the reality of the job ahead begins to sink in relatively quickly.

Whether you are in a safe seat, a marginal, or an unwinnable, the main overarching goal for the candidate is the same: Do not make a balls of it.

It is too easy to get sucked into the excitement of a General Election and actually think that much of what you say or do can have much of a positive impact on the outcome of the campaign – but if you say the wrong thing, it may not only run in your local media but be picked up by the wider national media. For example, you may think you are being particularly clever and astute, sticking up for local residents, by telling the Sheffield Star newspaper that you are going to tell your party leader that if he doesn't listen to you over who runs your local library then there will be trouble – but when they then sell this on to a range of national titles under the headline *"Leading candidate tells PM he has lost plot over libraries"*, you will feel less good.

Most media generally have an obligation to give balance to their reporting during a General Election campaign. In practice, this means giving each candidate an equal amount of bad press, whilst reprinting a photo of them all eating candy floss at a local fete. Balance is subjective, but on the whole, most local media, TV and radio will at least tip their hat at giving everyone a fair run. National newspapers less so – they can write whatever they like, they can pick a favourite and do down the opposition without having to worry about something as trivial as fair and balanced election coverage. For example, I doubt anyone would describe The Sun's 1992 election day attack on Neil Kinnock, *"The Welsh Windbag"*, as a particularly balanced one: *"If Kinnock wins today, will the last person to leave Britain please turn out the lights."* It's not as if he needed any help with throwing the election away at this point, but it was nice for The Sun to lend him a hand anyway.

Most candidates are selected around 18 months to two years ahead of the General Election. The main parties like to have candidates in post well ahead of election day in order to give them some traction and voter recognition ahead of the vote. They want candidates to show up at all the local events, knock on doors and leaflet people into submission.

The only time when this is not the case is when an MP stands down at the very last minute and a replacement must be found urgently. What is interesting about such appointments is that usual selection processes are suspended and the national party allowed to put in their own candidate. A cynic might think that such arrangements could be open to manipulation – for example, a veteran MP could be persuaded the time is right to move into the House of Lords and then their seat can be utilized for the party's Special Advisor of choice. There is an interesting section in Chris Mullin's book where a young David Miliband is persuaded to become an MP, when he really would rather prefer to stay being an advisor. In such circumstances, when your candidate being appointed a few weeks before the poll and does not have time to be properly scrutinised or have name recognition etc, can be seen as quite a good thing. At most elections, despite my keen interest in such things, there will be one or two people who are drafted in at the last minute who creep under my radar. I am there looking at the paper a month or so after the election saying: *"Hey, when did **they** become an MP?"*

As we touched on in the previous chapter, at a standard General Election (if there is such a thing), very few seats will change hands. As a candidate, your job is to hold the fort and not give in to the inevitable.

For most of us mere mortals, we will be fighting unwinnable seats. Although we cannot call them that. We have to pretend that, due to our hard work and diligence, we can turn round any hopeless cause.

What separates the relatively sane candidates from the delusional, is that we know our place in the scheme of things. Ours is not to reason why, ours is but to do or die. (Actually, ours is always to die without reasoning why.) We know that fighting an unwinnable is good experience (in the sense of looking impressive on our CV, as opposed to in the sense of being enjoyable) and that our role is to draw some fire away from genuinely winnable seats.

However there will be many first time candidates who believe their own hype. They genuinely believe they can turn around a 10,000 majority by visiting the local fete, putting a letter in the local paper about pot holes and by contacting every person in their key wards 7 times before election day.

My experience from canvassing a variety of wards in local, European and General Elections is that it is rarely a lack of canvass information that will cost you a seat in an opponent's electoral heartland – generally it will be due to a lack of people wanting to vote for you and your party in that area. To put it plainly, I can knock every house in Henley-Upon-Thames 7 times over, asking them to vote for the socialists, but all that will happen is that I am told 7 times by someone's butler to get lost.

With the advent of social media, the battle for hearts and minds has taken on new forms. You know that very few voters in your ward are likely to be reading your Twitter/Facebook/blog account, but what you do know is that the one group certain to be monitoring your every word will be your electoral opponents. And thus the game begins.

A quick glance at Twitter ahead of a key election is almost as funny as it is tedious. Scores of candidates and party workers telling you that they have just spent a *"fantastic"* 2 hours in the rain getting *"a great response"* in such and such ward, whilst out canvassing. Every single entry will follow the above format.

Having been on hundreds of canvassing sessions in various different places, a more accurate response is likely to be along the lines of: *"Only 3 of us turned up (the candidate, me and the candidate's Mum), it rained consistently which really messed up all our leaflets, half the people were out (or pretending to be out), of those that opened the doors half told us to get lost or that they didn't vote, and 5 people we already knew were voting for us told us they would consider voting for us. We also got attacked by a little yapping dog, and at this point decided to give up and go to the pub."*

If you really were trying to dislodge an incumbent, what you would do is try to do a shed load of canvassing in areas you felt you can turn over through talking to local residents, but hope that your opposition remained unaware of this and carried on doing no work in that particular area, allowing you to pick up even more votes. The use of social media, channelling the spirit of the former Iraqi Information Minister (do you remember him saying *"There are no tanks here, everything is fine"* as the tanks rolled past him in the background of the camera shot) is simply a tactic to get under the skin of your opponents, goading them that you are significantly better and more organised than them. Most of your opposition candidates, if they are odds-on to win anyway, will simply ignore you and get on with what they are doing – any that are genuinely concerned will simply form a posse and hit the area you claim to have converted with renewed vigour to ensure that any waverers come back to the fold. As election campaigning tactics go, it's not the brightest.

Most first time General Election candidates do not understand election voting tactics and strategies though. They will have nodded sagely when during their candidates' briefings with the party, and other prospective candidates, when they have been told at election time resources will need to be targeted at key seats and that everyone will be expected to turn up and lend their support in those constituencies. What they have failed to grasp though is that the party official is speaking directly to them at this point and not to everyone else in the room. The delusional first time candidate honestly believes that their seat, the one that has never changed from being represented by the main opposition party in the history of the world, is a key seat and they are going to buck the national voting trends and deliver victory.

Some candidates can be taken quite by surprise when, a few weeks before polling day, they are told to stop working their own seat (-10,000 majority, but in the candidate's mind starting to look a bit wobbly) and told to go to the neighbouring constituency (-1,000 majority and narrowly lost at the last election), taking all their activists with them, and campaign for a colleague.

I have seen many spit the dummy, arguing how it is all going to be different this time, and that the party is fatally undermining local democracy. Many will continue to ignore the advice and continue solely working their own patch and forbidding their ragtag group of supporters to go anywhere remotely helpful – these are the people who immediately get a big black mark next to their name and a note taken at party HQ not to allow them near anything bordering on useful in the future.

I feel something bordering on admiration for the cynical old party hacks who work in the Regional HQs of our political parties. I mean they are as tough as old boots, have been round the block several times and are as wizened and gnarled as an old tree stubbornly clinging to a river bank, refusing to get swept away by the current – but they at least have a realistic pragmatic approach to life, unlike the idealistic fantasists who usually infest politics. I wonder if they take it in turns to phone up and berate candidates who are too self-absorbed to listen to reason – or whether this is seen as a perk of the job? All I do know is that following election day when the majority in this unwinnable has been cut to a far more manageable 9,000, they do not tend to phone up to gloat – which is just as well, because the candidate will probably still be sticking to their guns that they could have won the seat with a bit more support from the party and that they delivered the biggest swing (4%) in their region, so should now be given a safe seat out of gratitude for being so utterly brilliant.

If being involved in a political party is being part of an orchestra – everybody playing a small part in helping a bigger enterprise to flourish collectively – then being a Parliamentary candidate is the equivalent of being a one-man band.

(I will wait for the feminists reading the book get over the fact that I did not say *'one-person band'*, and then we can move on.)

Being a one-man band has its benefits and its drawbacks. You will be in demand, people will care about what you say and analyse your musings at length, the future (well at least the next 18 months) of your local party is in your hands. Feel the power. Equally, you can feel lonely, isolated and overwhelmed by the sheer task at hand, knowing that there is little you can do to realistically deliver lasting change.

Also one-man bands are rubbish, they make a bloody awful racket and create crowds outside tube stations which cause an annoying obstruction to those trying to go about their daily business. Clearly, this is a great analogy that works on several levels.

Even if you have never held public office before, you will soon learn how to speak and think like an established politician. Every sentence that trips off your lips is an opportunity to tell people how wonderful your party is and how rubbish the other parties are.

Politicians have a great ability to see everything in black and white. Every issue, every thought, every sentence. There are only two possible explanations for everything: 1) The right reason or solution – which only you can provide (even if it has been handed down to you via email that morning by the party's Communications Department in bite-size form, with a series of helpful attack lines and suggested quotes) and 2) The wrong reason or solution – which will be provided by your opponents and could lead to the destruction of the known world, or at least Armageddon down at the local Lidl.

One of the greatest failings of politics is the binary approach to every issue. Breaking news: Your opponents are not always wrong, they are not always nasty and they are not always doing everything simply to annoy you – or to take the country to Hell in a handcart.

It is not a failing to agree or to find consensus, but it is a great failing to find division where there is none and to deliberately misrepresent the views of your political opponents.

I have some sympathy with politicians when the media, which clearly has no agenda or opinion of its own to promote, ask simple *'Yes/No'* questions to which there is no appropriate answer. I can understand why politicians choose to give long rambling answers that deliberately cover all bases so that it makes it difficult for third parties to take sections out of context. I can understand why politicians will always try to focus on the positives of their ideology and strategy rather than allow themselves to just talk about the weak parts. However I have no sympathy whatsoever with people who deliberately mangle the truth for electoral gain.

As a Christian, perhaps I have a unique perspective that everyone should be allowed to be treated fairly, everyone should be allowed to speak for themselves and that everyone should be accountable for their own beliefs or actions. Maybe that's just a human thing, I don't know. But if someone's logic and ideology is so fundamentally flawed that everything they say could be used against them, simply allow them to be hoist by their own petard rather than climbing into the gutter with them to see who can throw the most mud.

Whilst there are parts of the campaign that are inevitably hard work – canvassing, casework, having to talk to real human beings – there are other parts which can be great fun. For me there were certain opportunities that I looked forward to and really helped to alleviate the trudge towards the inevitable.

Most of the local papers will do some kind of election feature. They feel this is their duty or obligation to the voters, but will usually do so in such a way that clearly indicates they couldn't give a monkey's about national politics. In other words, don't prepare yourself as if you were going for a Paxman style grilling on Newsnight, rather prepare as if Lorraine Kelly was going to have a lovely wee chat with you on the Daybreak sofa.

I can remember being asked such dynamite questions as: *"What newspapers do you read on a daily basis?", "Do you like football or rugby and, if so, what teams do you support?", "Why should people vote for you?"* – you felt it was one short step away from being asked what was your favourite colour, or who was your favourite Spice Girl.

The trick for the true politico is to turn this around to your own electoral benefit. For example, when asked what newspapers you read, tell them you read a wide variety (picking any one national title will imply that you hold the same political ideology or knee-jerk views to most issues) but the most important is your local paper [insert name here]. This will work well on two levels – firstly, it will make it seem that local issues and local people are far more important to you than what may be going on nationally; secondly, this will be appearing in that local paper and it will make it seem to readers of that newspaper that you are just like them. If you are asked for your favourite football team or rugby team – even though you hate all forms of sport or physical exercise and have done since you were a child – you say that you have been really struck since moving to the constituency how wonderful the local team is, you wish them every success and hope that results pick up for them soon because they (and their amazing supporters) really deserve it. You get the idea.

These are open-ended questions to which there is no right answer. You can waste a lot of time and energy thinking up suitable replies, but it does make a nice change to having your fingers nearly snapped off by creaky old letterboxes and the dogs that guard them.

The other great entertainment I found was attending local hustings events. Usually the hustings would be held in a local church hall, or school, or another community venue that sees it has a civic duty to engage with the political process. These events are an opportunity for local residents to come out and meet those putting themselves up for election (at least those who can be bothered to turn up to argue their case) and it is usually held in a format similar to that operated by BBC Question Time.

Sadly most constituencies will not be able to afford David Dimbleby, so the event will instead be chaired by some local volunteer who combines the key skills of being able to read questions that the audience has submitted in advance and who also has a fully functioning watch.

I can remember taking part in four local hustings events. Two full hustings held at either end of the constituency – both attended by around 100 people – and two youth hustings for people who did not have a vote, and would not have a vote in a General Election for another 5 years. I did particularly well in those debates given the fact it had absolutely no bearing whatsoever on the outcome of the election.

Maybe it's just that I enjoy the buzz of these encounters, knowing that you are living on your wits and one false move can bring the whole thing crashing down around you. It's the same feeling I get whenever I go to a really eerily quiet library or church and I get some urge from deep inside to shout something inappropriate really loudly – you don't do it because you know it would be seriously frowned upon, but that devil sitting on your shoulder is dying for you to do it, just once.

I've been a panellist on BBC Schools Question Time a handful of times. It's like a feeder version for the full BBC One event – schools competing to get the opportunity to be part of the production team for a one-off show later in the series. There are cameras, microphones and all sorts of things like that. The first one I took part in I was a last minute replacement for Keith Vaz, who had pulled out on the day – as the Leader of the local council's Labour Group, I was the obvious/cheapest/only person they could find at short notice*. (*Delete as appropriate.)

If I recall correctly, the mock-programme was hosted by David Dimbleby, and the other panellists were: George Galloway (Respect), Alan Duncan (Conservative), Daniel Finklestein (from The Times) and someone from Stop The War Coalition. I can't remember there being a Lib Dem, but there is every chance there was someone and I simply can't remember them because they were so utterly forgettable. It was great fun. George Galloway even told me I was much nicer than Keith Vaz, which I am still to this day trying to work out was some kind of backhanded compliment – but you've got to take praise wherever you can get it.

Election day itself is like a black dog that sits on your shoulder – is it me or are these analogies getting worse? You know it's there, you try and ignore it, but sooner or later it's going to bite your head off. Of course, if you are going to win then it's probably very exciting and you look forward to the day like you would to a child getting its presents at Christmas. For the rest of us, it's a fairly sombre experience, like a contractual obligation you have to fulfil – like a 70s rock band who are trying to promote a new album of work, but know they are going to have to do an encore where they do their one or two songs you've actually heard of. This particular election day fell ominously on 05/05/05 – the day when the black dog would inevitably bite.

The day before the election is known as the eve of poll. On the eve of poll and the day of poll, you will be running around like a headless chicken trying to eke out the last couple of potential votes from your core support or alternatively just trying to make it look like you are doing something vaguely useful. In most unwinnable seats you could just go down the pub and watch some international golf tournament and achieve much the same amount of success. Leaflets through letterboxes, special cardboard labels put on milk bottles (for the few people who still get their milk delivered at 5am by the milkman/milkperson/milkoperative* rather than just go to Tescos and stick it straight in the fridge) and any other gimmicks you can think of. I'd like to know exactly how much parties spend on pointless campaign gimmicks – you know the thing, a piece of card that when you move it in the light makes William Hague turn into Margaret Thatcher; a thing that you can stick on your phone that flashes a bit (just above where it says *'Vote Labour/Lib Dem/Tory**') but then packs up soon after you get a headache from your retinas having been burnt out; or a flag that you can hang out of your car window, but will buckle and fall out onto the road whenever you go over 20 mph. The genuinely extravagant ones, like Nigel Farage flying in a plane with giant *'Vote UKIP'* banner (before crashing into a field), I can kind of understand, but it's the sheer weight of tat that has been imported in from China for the occasion that gets me.

The old cliché about elections is that Conservative voters will go and vote first thing in the day. They'll sweep the leaves from their front steps, have a nice cup of tea and then be down the polling station straight away to uphold their moral duty to be an active part of the democratic process. Labour voters will turn up after work, in the evenings, if it isn't raining and if there isn't anything better on telly (e.g. Coronation Street/Eastenders – depending on whether they live in the North or South – or a sporting event involving England). And Lib Dem voters will turn up as soon as they can get their sandals on.

Whilst the above cliché is clearly told for comic effect, there is a grain of truth lying at the heart of it. The challenge for Labour in its heartlands is to *'get out the vote'* – encourage people to actually turn up and bother themselves to cast their ballot – this is why, where possible, you will see local activists trying to persuade people onto postal votes in order to increase the chances of someone actually voting. Conservatives do not tend to have the same problems to any great degree. Conservative voters will vote come rain, wind or shine – even if there is a plague of locusts they will be down there, pencil in hand. Conservatives have a significant rump of what we would call *'hard support'* and a small amount of *'soft support'* – for Labour it is the other way around, which is why they have more waverers to win over. Canvassing simply allows you to focus on winning the waverers – if someone is definitely voting for you, there is no need to waste too much time going backwards and forwards checking that's still the case; same goes for people who tell you to get stuffed, if they are definitely not voting for you, cross them off the list and move onto the next house – focus on the people who can still be persuaded/convinced.

In a General Election, Polls open at 7am and close at 10pm. If you are a candidate there is some expectation that you will turn up to attend the count – but it is not obligatory. When I stood there was a candidate for one of the smaller parties who turned up for 10 minutes, almost to check the count was actually happening, and then went home. Perhaps he genuinely thought he could win and a short glance at a sample returns suggested otherwise, I don't know.

At 10pm on the dot, people will be tuned into one of the main news channels to hear their take on what is about to happen. This may seem slightly odd, but during the hours of polling the TV and radio news are not allowed to report on the election – aside from saying that it is happening and that polls are open – for weeks in the run up to the election every word, sigh and frown is reported and analysed at great length, but on the day itself there will be nothing that might influence the voters until the last vote has been cast. During the day the media will be conducting their own exit polls – basically asking people, on their way out from voting, who they voted for. It's not an exact science but by 10pm they will have a good idea how the election is likely to go.

There will be seats where there are local exceptions to the national swing – particularly seats where there may be a large Lib Dem presence to defend – but on the whole most seats will conform to the national swing, which again underlines the true pointlessness of most candidates to the process.

Most candidates will watch the 10pm news at home. There's little point turning up to the election count directly at the close of polls because the ballot boxes will need to be sealed and then transported back from across the constituency to the central count. That can take some time.

The count will normally be held somewhere like the local town hall, but in my case it was a local leisure centre. An empty and fairly soulless community building, which made you feel that you and the few others present (candidates, tellers/party workers and media) had been quarantined in this big empty glass structure after an outbreak of something particularly horrid in the locality. And that's just the start of the evening. You might have 7 or 8 hours of this to endure.

I tried to put on a brave face, safe in the knowledge that I knew the result even before I turned up – but given that my day job at this time was also in politics, I had been rather distracted by the fact that the MP who employed me was also contesting his marginal seat at the same time, on the other side of the country.

I would periodically walk around the badminton and basketball courts looking at the votes stacking up – mainly for everyone else – and would then find myself being inevitably drawn back to the sofas in reception where a single small TV screen displayed the results coming in from up and down the country. This was perhaps a natural yearning considering it was matters elsewhere which would determine whether I still had a job or not.

There is something surreal about sitting in an empty leisure centre while your life (or at least the bits of your life that you are paid for) flashes before your eyes. You are trying to analyse 100 pieces of information at once, just in case that short one second piece of tickertape at the bottom of the screen flashes *'HOLD'* and you can relax, or *'GAIN'* and you immediately need to dig out the Guardian Jobs section.

Just before 5am, there was a general hubbub and the candidates were encouraged to go through to the main hall – a declaration was on the horizon, as was the dawn sun.

Having been up for over 24 hours by this point, and not knowing whether I would be able to pay the bills come the next day due to the possibility of losing my employment, I have to say I had little interest in the traditional pastime of arguing over whether a handful of votes had in fact been spoilt or not.

I understand the importance of spoilt votes in a close contest. In council elections they can mean the difference between winning and losing. Some contests have been decided by pulling lots or tossing a coin – one vote could be decisive. I mean, it probably won't be, but it might be. Whole teams of nerds crouch over the count to see if one solitary vote has been put in the wrong pile, and if they see such an horrendous turn of events they will shout the house down as if the whole of modern democracy has been brought down around our ears. Only if it benefits their candidate though. That's why I am rubbish at such things, my innate sense of fair play means I am equally likely to point out that a vote has been accidentally put in our pile when it should have gone to our opponent.

Then again, if as in this case, the overall majority is something approaching 8,500 votes, then it really makes no difference.

What are the odds of two parliamentary seats on other sides of the country declaring at exactly the same time? One a marginal seat, one a safe seat. In Sunderland they have it all done in around an hour, they bring in the ballot boxes in vans and then people in brightly coloured sweatshirts and baseball caps push the votes into the counting hall in shopping trolleys, where a conveyer belt of clerks from the local bank rack up the scores in record time. I'm not even joking. It's like a bad episode of Supermarket Sweep. Sadly I was not standing in Sunderland – this is mostly sad because I may have actually won that seat.

However at 5am the die was cast – metaphorically, not literally, if our seat had ended up a tie, I may have called for a recount myself. Actually, I wouldn't have done, because that probably would have kept me from my bed for another couple of hours. The Conservatives had won my home seat with a grand total of 23,494 votes (it could have been 23,495 votes if the Spoilt paper that said *"F*** Off BNP scum"* had been counted in their favour, but such is life), the Lib Dems polled 15,021 votes and I had 10,466 votes. I am still surprised that nearly ten and a half thousand people bothered to vote for me, but I am reassured that they would have been equally likely to vote for a trained macaw called Maurice – indeed, this could have boosted support significantly. At least I didn't finish last. Thank God for UKIP (and it's not often you will hear me say that) who racked up 1,107 votes.

Would I do it again? Possibly. Would I be allowed to do it again? Probably not.

All I know is that my boss held on with a majority of 1,996, and that meant I could go and buy a bacon sandwich.

7. Post Election

Following an election, particularly a General Election, there will be many things that a politician wants to do. Foremost amongst these will be to sleep for a few days.

You may think that all politicians, at least the winning ones, would feel invigorated and energised by the democratic process – they have been given a renewed mandate to change the world (or not change the world depending on their political perspective). You might think that there is nothing that they would rather do than get straight back to work and put the world to rights. You would be wrong.

The political spin machines may tell you that it's just a normal day back at the office and that the work of government carries on as usual, but this is only partly correct. It is correct in that the civil servants are still there in true *Yes Minister* style, regardless of who has won, keeping the wheels of power turning – but most of the politicians, Prime Minister aside, will be getting some much needed shut-eye.

The General Election will have taken place on a Thursday and then most of the politicians – the ones not doing the rounds of the TV studios in Westminster – will come back to Parliament the next Tuesday or Wednesday to start afresh.

There is a need for some perspective in these matters – aside from the physical rigours that candidates will have undergone, there are great mental pressures too. Entire careers and reputations can be destroyed overnight. Most candidates and their closest supporters will have worked over a 24-hour day on Polling Day itself, but in the days and weeks before the election the demands will have been equally strenuous.

Now reflect that most politicians in marginal seats will have been actively campaigning for the 18 months, if not longer, before Polling Day trying to put out a coherent message whilst destroying all local opposition at the same time. It can take its toll.

Now just imagine if you lose!

History is littered with examples of one-term MPs who on getting into Parliament – maybe unexpectedly, but almost always on a wafer-thin majority – are then promptly dispatched next time around with having achieved very little at all.

Partly people in this position may be immobilised through fear – one false move could cost their job. Partly it might be that, to use a gambling expression, they feel they are on some kind of *'free roll'* – they never expected to be here, they probably won't get elected again, so they might as well enjoy the perks and the celebrity whilst they can.

The comedown is far worse for people who never expected to lose their seat – especially if they have been an MP for many years and don't know what to do next. With our increasingly professionalised Parliament, increasingly inhabited by career politicians who have not known employment outside of politics or the coat-tails of the Westminster Bubble, what do you do when the general public gives you the thumbs down? What if you have no other expertise or vocation to fall back on?

Do you expect people to feel sorry for you? A quick flick back to that memorable night in

1997, the landslide result that defined a generation of Government to come, tells you that there is little compassion or sympathy shown to losers. With Government Ministers losing what were thought of as *'safe'* seats, left, right and centre, there was nowhere to hide.

Some take it better than others. David Mellor in Putney got into an unsightly and unbecoming spat with The Reform Party candidate Sir James Goldsmith, as the Labour candidate no-one remembers (Tony Colman, if you are interested) crept in with a majority nearing 3,000 votes.

Or did you *"stay up for Portillo"* (something that political hacks now do regularly, as he sits on the BBC This Week sofa late on a Thursday night), when he was ousted by fresh-faced candidate Stephen Twigg? No fireworks here, as Portillo swallowed his pride and adopted a brave face like a man standing on the scaffold waiting to be put out of his misery, but it was deeply uncomfortable nonetheless. The audible laughter and giggles as Portillo went through the formality of having his full name and votes tally read out – *"Michael Denzil Xavier Portillo,*

Conservative Party, 19,137 votes" – was (let's face it) amusing, if borderline xenophobic given his Spanish roots. I felt sorry for the guy. Even hate figures must have feelings too.

What do you do next having suffered such ignominy? It seems in many cases – for those not buckling down to give re-election another shot (cf Ken Livingstone versus Boris Johnson as Mayor of London) – that the obvious choice is to take a turn in the media spotlight in a slightly different capacity. Usually this will be as a talking head on issues of politics, or on gameshows like *Have I Got News For You*, but in other cases it might be to reinvent yourself entirely.

You may not have heard of Dick Tuck (you may even think that he sounds like a particularly intimate surgical operation), but you will have heard of his great political aphorism: *"The people have spoken, the bastards."* Once the public has had its say, you need to take the verdict on the chin and try to move on.

To pick the two examples I highlighted from the 1997 General Election: David Mellor took his seat behind the Radio 5 Live 606 broadcasting mic – deciding that arguing the toss over sport with the public was far preferable than arguing the toss with them over politics. As a former Minister of Sport he was ably qualified, and – for all his faults – he remained an engaging and entertaining speaker people didn't mind listening to. Portillo had something of a Damascene conversion, ditching the hard-line exterior he had once taken on to instead reinvent himself as much more reasonable, more humble, more human human-being. He started making programmes with the BBC and Channel 4, focussing on things such as families living on the breadline in Liverpool, and talked about how he had had homosexual experiences at school. Was it just a clever game? In 1999 he would return to politics in this new form at a by-election in Kensington and Chelsea, and re-establishing himself as a potential Conservative leader of the future. However having lost out to Iain Duncan Smith (and Ken Clarke, having finished third) in the party's leadership ballot, he voluntarily quit as an MP and went back to television. On top of his *This Week* employment, he is also now famed for his travel programmes about The Great British

Railways that appear on the BBC, which focus on the history of the train network in the UK and further afield.

For others, the transition is not so easy. Lib Dem MP Lembit Opik had always seemed to enjoy the TV circuit when an MP. You might have seen him on things like *Have I Got News For You* (indeed, he also appeared the day after losing his seat in the 2010 General Election), *All Star Mr and Mrs* and Ant and Dec vehicles such as *Saturday Night Takeaway* and *I'm A Celebrity Get Me Out Of Here*. He had had high profile romances, notably with TV weather presenter Sian Lloyd and Gabriele Irimia (one half of The Cheeky Girls). He decided on leaving Parliament that he would give stand-up comedy a go. Whilst the words *"frying pan"* and *"fire"* spring to mind, good on him for putting himself out there. His debut, witnessed by a helpful BBC journalist, was described as *"not fantastic, but not completely awful"* which isn't exactly a ringing endorsement you'd want put on the posters under your name.

There is an expectation by those outside the political process, that those that lose their seats will be OK. Again this is probably because we do not see them as living, breathing politicians, but rather as organs of a disconnected political elite working under a corrupt system. We see them almost as collateral damage – a way of giving the Prime Minister of the day a bloody nose – they will no doubt find themselves a cushy job within politics, the media or in a private sector role. Friends in high places, and all that. For some the truth can be very different.

Whilst there are no shortage of MPs who bag lucrative jobs in the media or in the political frontline in another way (for example in a newly created position in the House of Lords), or miraculously find employment in one consultancy or another, or in a highly paid position in an organisation like the BBC, there are also many former MPs who must feel like they are on the employment scrapheap.

Following the 2005 election, I spoke with one MP who had just lost his seat a couple of months before. I was sat next to him in a curry house in Bradford, trying to make small talk, without discussing the proverbial elephant in the room. He cut an isolated and sombre figure and understandably wasn't much up for shooting the breeze with a bunch of politicos. Before long, the person opposite blundered in with both feet, asking what this poor guy was doing now, post Parliament. He looked up forlornly, shrugged, and looked back at his curry. He said he didn't know what he was going to do now and was waiting to hear back on a job application he had recently submitted to become a local bus driver. It was a bit of a comedown, but he had found that every other option he had tried seemed to be a closed shop. I am happy to say that (having now Googled the person in question) he instead eventually went into a freelance consultancy role and then back into academia/education – where his career had laid pre-Parliament. It's a tough world, and no-one owes you a living.

Losing must be particularly hard to take at elections where most of your party colleagues were re-elected, and you have been dealt a knockout blow.

The Tuesday after the 2001 General Election, I was stood on Whitehall preparing myself to go back to work. As I stood there, an MP I knew relatively well walked past. I stopped him and said it was good to see him. He asked how the election had gone and I said:

"It went well. At least we all got back in." At that moment his face turned ashen and I realised that the person stood opposite had clearly just lost something of an epic battle.

In a Parliament of over 650 constituencies, it's easy to miss election results – even of people you know and like. But suffice it to say, I felt a bit of git. This guy probably felt that I had seen the result and was taking the rise out of him. Having gone back to my office and checked this particular result, I saw that he had suffered a 1.1% swing – enough to lose the election by 383 votes. Poor soul. (He'd subsequently stand in a Scottish Parliament seat and lose to the wife of the man who had ousted him from Westminster. Perhaps he walked under a ladder once…I certainly wouldn't get him to pick my lottery numbers.)

So why come back to Parliament if you've lost? During the election campaign, the MPs' offices within Parliament are locked. As soon as the election is called, everyone is turfed out and relocates to their constituencies. The main reason for this is so that incumbents do not get an unfair advantage (at the taxpayer's expense).

Even outside of election times, you are not meant to undertake party political work on Parliamentary computers, phones or photocopiers. It's a grey area, but it is mostly respected. You will see some MPs in marginal seats choosing to have constituency based community-facing workers rather than administrative or research staff in Westminster. It's much harder to keep tabs on what happens out in the constituencies, but it is understood Parliamentary resources should not be used for overt campaigning.

Most MPs will not believe they are going to lose their seats, even if all the polls tell them that this is the likely outcome. This often leaves an awkward moment post-election when the Serjeant at Arms needs the office back and it is full up with someone else's files and personal belongings.

Usually the Serjeant at Arms will play a softly softly catchy monkey approach. On a human level, when someone has had their world destroyed, the last thing they want is to be told to come and clear their office. This often means the process can go on for weeks.

Some MPs, like the one I bumped into, will simply choose to come in at the first possible opportunity and put everything in a bin. This gives them some sort of closure and they can move on. Others will simply bury their head in the sand and pretend that nothing has happened – perhaps they were never an MP after all and it had all been a bad dream? The problem with this latter approach is that there are a limited number of offices in Parliament. This means that many newbie MPs will be left weeks working without an office, trying to conduct their business from a locker or the Portcullis House eLibrary.

Other MPs, the more astute, who see that their time in Parliament is about to expire, take some pleasure in shredding, binning and burning everything in their offices in the weeks before the election is likely to be called. Cathartic maybe, but hardly a good use of Parliamentary time.

For those MPs who are re-elected, the monotony begins again. The ever moving treadmill of life with demands on you from all around – your party, your constituents, the media. It's a back to school feel, but after one of those really long and tiring Summer holidays where you feel so exhausted you want to have another holiday just to recover.

The new MPs will probably have some energy to spare. Excited that they are going to change the country for the better – they will tell the whips, and the media, and everyone else, what for. They have put the world to rights many times down the pub with their supporters, and now their time has come. Give it 4 weeks and they'll be toeing the line, just like their predecessors, in the vain hope of being given a junior ministerial brief.

For the newbies, it's not so much back to school, more first day at university. Various orientation sessions will be set up in the Committee Rooms to help bring them up to speed and tell them where everything is in Parliament. All they really need to know is that they won't have an office for quite a while yet, and certainly not that big one overlooking the River Thames in Portcullis House that they actually want. As far as I am aware there isn't an equivalent of Freshers' Fair – where people give away bags of condoms and Super Noodles to MPs, whilst various Parliamentary Societies encourage others to join the Parliamentary Choir or the Lords beat-boxing team*. Westminster is probably a poorer place for this – but I can imagine the inevitable downing of shots in the Sports and Social could get a bit messy. (*This probably doesn't exist, but it really should.)

For some the new dawn is just beginning. For others the end has come. I can almost hear Elton John singing *'Circle of Life'* as I type. All we do know is that things will never be the same again.

8. Political Blogging

During the General Election of 2005 – an experience I have now tried to blot from my mind, through a combination of expensive counselling and very cheap whisky – I had struck upon the idea of running a political blog.

I'd like to pretend that this was determined effort to access hard-to-reach voters throughout the constituency I was contesting, but actually I thought it a great way to annoy my opponents.

I've mentioned previously the important role social media can play in pretending your campaign is being a lot more successful than it actually is. Every canvassing session is *"fantastic"* and gets *"an amazing response"*. (If you can get the hashtag *"#GameOn"* in there, so much the better.) This may not really be the case but it will make your campaign look 13% more capable and credible than it actually is.

Blogging an election campaign takes this delusion to the next level. Blogging allows you to get your message out to *'the people'* without being watered down by those with their own agenda, such as the press. It's democracy in action. Etc. If you really want to contact your voters and get them out to the ballot box, what it really is is a waste of time – the only people reading your blog are your political opponents (desperate for any slip up you might be stupid enough to make) and possibly your mum, if she's worked out how to use the internet yet.

However, there are ways of using this to your advantage.

Being a local councillor, as well as a Parliamentary candidate, I would be out at some worthy/boring meeting nearly every night of the week – even at weekends. So what I would do is every night tell my follower/s what I had been up to. I would then slip in what a great disappointment that my opponents weren't there. Clearly they were not interested in housing/residents' associations/pot holes/the state of bus shelters in Barton Way. Whilst this may well have been true, I suspect what my opponents were actually doing was (instead of being a glorified social-worker-come-professional-meeting-attender) going around delivering leaflets and knocking on doors. The fools.

Blogging a campaign is the political equivalent of tapping someone on the shoulder when they are trying to work on something really important. You might not be achieving much, but they won't be either because they'll be so distracted by you.

I had secured the catchy web address http://www.swherts.labour.co.uk/ViewPage.cfm?Page=12081 and was sure that it was only a matter of time before the world turned on its own axis. Hold on it does that anyway, doesn't it? I mean it turns the other way on its axis, the way it's not meant to.

Around a month after the General Election, where I was shocked to find that South West Hertfordshire was not quite ready to become a socialist republic (keep pushing, I am sure it's only a matter of time…2020 maybe?), I decided that if I was going to be pointlessly annoying, I may as well do it properly.

Having packed up the campaign blog, I had been contacted by a handful of people who had enjoyed reading it (seriously, get out more!) and wanted to know if I was going to write anything further. At the same time, one of my friends had begun his own political blog.

As all good friends should, when you see someone else having a good idea, steal it, adapt it and pass it off as your own brain wave. It's the same principle that explains why we have half a dozen programmes that look exactly the same as *Bargain Hunt* or *Come Dine With Me*.

So many inventors in recent history did not actually invent the products they are famous for. Often they simply had the money to take out the patent or the wherewithal to adapt someone else's basic idea into one that actually worked. In this context, it's not plagiarism; it's survival of the fittest. God bless Charles Darwin/Margaret Thatcher.

Anyway, having read the blog in question, I humbly thought: 1) I can do this better; 2) It can be a vehicle for me to write creatively about politics; 3) It can be a vehicle for me to vent my spleen at how nonsensical the political process can be; and 4) I really have nothing better to do with my time because I do not have a Nintendo Wii.*

(*Incidentally the first time I saw a Nintendo Wii was during Half Time at a football match at Vicarage Road, when the aforementioned company decided to give one away to the winner of a simple competition. Basically, two people had been pulled from the crowd and asked to play a game of Wii tennis whilst the teams were having their well-earned cup of tea *("milk, two sugars, don't bother me with discussion of the free kick routine now, I am in my special place")*. None of us had seen a Wii before, none of us understood the general concept, and – more to the point – none of us could really see what was going on. What we could see were two grown men stood on the halfway line waving their hands around crazily as if they were either trying to communicate to the crowd via semaphore or were trying to bat away a really angry swarm of midges. It looked fun, but not something that would catch on. How wrong we were.)

For most people starting a new website, the difficulty is finding a domain name that is striking, memorable and not already taken. Calling your website www.johnsmith38.com is not really going to help you in the long run. (Apologies if there genuinely is a John Smith out there with this domain – I am sure the work you are doing there is fantastic and recognition by the industry, whatever industry it is you are in, is just around the corner. Go you.)

When trying to secure a unique domain it is therefore the one occasion in life when having an extremely unusual name is a help rather than a hindrance. www.kerroncross.blogspot.com was born and I gave it the clever title *"Kerron Cross – Voice of the Delectable Left"*.

The title was meant to be tongue in cheek, a pun on the phrase *"The Voice of the Electable Left"*. Sadly, no-one has ever heard this phrase coined, as I expect that I may have invented it (although I have not paid for a patent yet, so if you can get in quick, it could be yours).

The Voice of the Electable Left is a phrase used by people when they are describing those who hold the most worthy/credible/left of centre views in any debate or conversation. You'll see it on *Question Time*, when someone who writes for the Independent (smaller readership than the Yorkshire Post, incidentally) tells you how we need to do more for the working classes – they will try and sing up their own credentials, like an old post-Marxist university lecturer, whilst desperately trying to conceal that they grew up in a very posh middle class suburb, went to a very good school and then onto Oxbridge, from where they got a writing junket in a paper nobody reads and even less pay any attention to. Who knows, one day they may graduate to writing for The Guardian.

Any such conversation which involves two people who claim to be the real voice of the left or the working masses tends to quickly degenerate into a variant of that old Monty Python sketch about the four Yorkshireman.

In our version within Parliament, it seems most of us grew up in an environment where we had to work 28 hour days, get up 4 hours before we went to bed and live with our family in a smartie tube on the M25.

Personally I used to dream of being able to live in a smartie tube*.

You get the idea.

(*It's worth mentioning for fellow pedants that smartie, as in a tube of smarties, is spelt *'smartie'* and not *'smarty'*. And as that is at least 5 mentions of the aforementioned chocolate product I will expect some to be delivered in the post pretty soon.)

So the *"Delectable Left"*, was meant to be a self-effacing joke based around this tradition, but also referencing how boring my voice sounds.

I'm quite fortunate/unfortunate that I tend to pick up accents of people that I spend too much time with. My Mum is Manx – a nation which is famously supposed to be accent-less, in the same way that people from Morningside in Edinburgh think they are accent-less. My Dad is from Wigan where they are somewhat less accent-less. I've worked in the Home Counties, in London, in Leicestershire, in Manchester and Yorkshire – to be honest, my accent is all over the place.

Somewhere in the genes I've picked up the ability to forget what my voice sounds like – on the radio I apparently bore for Britain in a Ken Livingstone-esque whiney South East

English tone, in real life most people seem to think I am from somewhere in the Midlands.

People used to come up to me and say things like: *"You have a good image for politics, I mean you're young, you're not bad looking and you seem to make sense."* I know that in reality I look a bit like a book worm and sound like Red Ken on one of his less interesting days. I will not be seduced by this faint praise.

Anyway, it's not difficult to look photogenic in politics, or to be young – or even to make sense, if you ignore the party media briefings.

Within a few months I had already built up something of a reputation for writing humorous postings about politics and the inner workings of Parliament. I think there were a couple of main reasons for this.

Politicians, and those who aspire to be politicians, are pretty risk averse. They want to be taken seriously and have taken years cultivating a persona that says they can tackle any issue without smirking – even if someone talks about *"a significant murmur in the lobbies"*. They are not about to risk this reputation by putting something in the public domain which can be latched onto by their opponents, or by the media, to destroy this credibility. Humour can make you seem more human, but it also brings with it risks – fallibility might be charming, but it can also weaken you at your foundations, if you are not careful. No-one wants to be on the wrong side of the media, or the whips, or the electorate.

Another person you do not want to be on the wrong side of is the Serjeant at Arms, therefore blogging about the internal workings of Parliament has its dangers too.

I couldn't have cared less about either of these things. I was a local councillor and, unless I said anything particularly daft or explosive, there was little the party could do to stop me from standing again so long as I kept my local party and members onside. They could stop me standing for Parliament again, sure, but given all the barriers already in place to stop people like me from getting near a winnable seat, it didn't seem like much to be giving up. Most political parties crave control, they do not want people going off doing and saying their own thing, even if they are right.

Oddly, being a passable blogger of passable note, I would get booked every now and then to go on national radio or TV to be a talking head. I realised that this was usually not to do with how funny or insightful my comments were, but rather that producers are up against deadlines and when needing political balance, if you live or work near a TV studio so you can come in at short notice, you will be first port of call because it stops them having to spend 2 hours phoning people they might actually want but logistically cannot get.

I wondered how much it would annoy the party to be coming up with supportive sound-bites and arguments on national media platforms but without having seen a party media briefing or having the first clue about what the approved line to take for the day was. *"Yes, it's a very good point, but it's not our point! We should be talking about the importance of the inner workings of the discussions at Davos"*, they might say.

I have never written anything that was deliberately hurtful or that was aimed at bringing down someone's career. There are plenty of political blogs which do this, and it's not for me. My musings were always meant to be a bit of fun, critiquing and satirising the stupidity of the political system, wherever your ideology sits in the current worldview. It wasn't a case of wanting to name and shame, or wanting people to lose their job, it was about allowing people to laugh at themselves and the ridiculous situations their chosen career perpetuates. *The Thick of It* does this caricaturing brilliantly, I guess I would like my blog to be seen of in a similar way – but put together by the writers of the *Carry On* films, rather than Armando Ianucci.

Being in the right place at the right time is everything in politics, as well as in life. Working within the Westminster Bubble, inside Parliament, I was always at the heart of democracy – in other words, if there was a protest or major incident, I could run downstairs and take a quick picture to put on my blog.

Not that this would be the sort of event that I would regularly cover. I would take far more inspiration from the state of the Parliamentary toilets (I was convinced for a long time that someone was living on our corridor, given that they had brought in not only their shampoo and conditioner but also left their toothbrush, towel and special scented soap in the bathroom too); the silly signs people would put on their doors or in the kitchen areas asking people not to do something really irritating like use the wrong mug (using an MP's special mug is actually a capital offence in some countries – it may seem harsh, but it cuts reoffending rates); or when someone in the Parliamentary Works Department would channel MacGyver and develop a construction out of a fork, a bucket and a tonne of duct tape to create a temporary fix for a leaky window.

We all need a laugh, to embrace the ridiculous and to celebrate the absurd. Perhaps that explains why I took that suicide mission to preach socialist values to the good people of Hertfordshire – I had previously thought it was to do with a misplaced sense of duty – but I'm happy to adopt any defence which helps cover up the fact that I didn't have any better options up my sleeve.

Couple this with an interest in local government, the church, football and all things Watford FC, and I had developed a sweet little niche for myself.

Serjeant at Arms never bothered with me – even though I did undermine all the edicts about not taking photos within Parliament and also got some coverage in the national press about the inherent bias in the system where one set of rules apply to MPs and another to everyone else.* It's almost like the Serjeant had better things to do. Incredible, I know.

(*One memorable story surrounded an incident during the 2002 World Cup, where an event for researchers and secretaries to watch England versus Argentina during recess was cancelled by the House authorities, as it was deemed not to be an appropriate use of Parliamentary resources. Indeed all the rooms large enough to host such an event were locked on the day in question to stop anyone holding their own informal gathering. However the event for the MPs to watch England versus Nigeria, a week or so later, was deemed an appropriate use of resources – despite protests from staff inside Parliament. It is not so much what you do in Parliament but who you are. I am almost glad that the England-Nigeria result turned out to be a very dull 0-0.)

Word of mouth, and sporadic media appearances, ensured that pretty soon my blog had at least come to the attention of those within the political blogging community. By the end of 2006 I had been awarded the coveted title of *"Labour's Best Political Blogger"*. Obviously I was very flattered and embarrassed in equal measure.

It is probably worth mentioning that I didn't win any sort of popular vote to receive the title, it was based around the judgements and selections of prominent writer, blogger, media talking-head, publisher and former Conservative Parliamentary Candidate, Iain Dale. I guess it's how people at the Mercury Prize feel after a committee of the great and good decide to give you the recognition they feel you deserve, whilst other acts have to go out and win over large chunks of the public to win something. What I am saying is, it was no Smash Hits Poll Winners' Party – but hopefully this doesn't mean the award lacked credibility or wasn't deserved/appreciated/meaningful.

Of course, you could say *"Labour's Best Political Blogger 2006"* loosely translates into English as: *"Didn't win it the last 8 years"*. That's a fair comment, I suppose. (I will be sure to bring this up next time anyone talks about the England football team as world beaters, due to them having won the World Cup in 1966.) Although in fairness to me, I did quit blogging in 2009, and the period in the intervening years the selection process moved from being the choice of Iain alone to a public vote – which severely hampered my chances. I still finished in the top 3 most years though, which was nice.

I no longer feel the need to write long diatribes on a blog anymore, I've grown out of this. That's what books are for, right? And if you can condense it all down to 140 characters, you're laughing (even if no-one else is) thanks to Twitter.

No longer will I have to spend hours and hours of my day writing three or four carefully crafted posts about the future of our democracy, our country, our place in the global hierarchy.

No, thankfully, I can now do my toilet jokes and double entendres* in a fraction of the time via my iPhone. (*Though I can usually only give you a small one.)

There's all this tosh about bloggers being *'citizen journalists'*, due to the fact most young professionals have access to internet enabled technology, but actually we are all just passing the time making life interesting for ourselves. The more hard-core amongst us might believe we can change the world via our musings, or that a journalistic career might be around the corner – but it's just a middle class version of that disease where people who audition for X Factor think that this will transform their lives for the better. Blogging rarely achieves anything in, or of, itself.

However, when Twitter start giving political awards for micro-blogging, I'm sure I'll be at the front of the queue. It's only a matter of time. This time next year Rodney, we'll be millionaires.

9. Influencing the Political Process

"If voting changed anything they would make it illegal", so said Emma Goldman, a Lithuanian born American international anarchist. I bet she was a real laugh at dinner parties.

This populist sentiment of non-participation has always lurked under the surface in British politics, but seems to be coming into the consciousness more prevalently thanks to visionary intellectuals and thinkers such as Russell Brand.

Russell is a man eager to tell us what he thinks about how corrupt the political process is – you would have thought from his tone that his experience is based on finding that, despite repeatedly trying to get rid of politicians he disagrees with at the ballot box, he has decided voting changes nothing. But no, Russell has never voted, not once, in any election.

I never understand the sentiment that says there is no point in voting because bad people/people you disagree with/people who are all the same* will get in. Even if this sweeping generalisation was true, surely the sensible response would be to get *more* involved, rather than leave the decision-making process to someone else entirely. One thing is true in politics: if you do not speak up for yourself, someone will speak for you.

It's not like withdrawing your vote is going to change anything. It's not like David Cameron, Ed Miliband and Nick Clegg are sat there thinking: *"Well, Joe Bloggs in Nuneaton couldn't be bothered to vote, we'll have to restructure the whole way we do politics now to ensure he's included next time."*

Total non-participation in the democratic process shows a lack of imagination, a lack of hope, and a lack of reasoned thinking. If you really wanted to stick it to those out of touch/lazy/money-grabbing politicians*, then what better way than to vote them out? Sitting on your hands is exactly what they *want* you to do.

You don't have to hold a private hustings to know what your candidates think. All candidates' addresses are listed on the notice of election – and most candidates will put leaflets through your door with their phone number on. Why not spend 30 seconds of your busy life to ask them what they think on the matters that are important to you?

Also, if you do not communicate what the big issues are from your perspective, how can you hope that they will be reflected in the policy-making of the main parties?

I'm involved in the political process, I'm even a member of a political party, but unlike some of the zealots you might come across (normally powered by a will to get on, rather than any deep-seated belief in anything too ideological) I recognise that no political party or politician is ever going to be right 100% of the time – they are even less likely to agree with my views 100% of the time – but that's why politics needs to be open and why we need healthy debates about the important issues of the day.

Have I disagreed with my party before? Yes. I publicly spoke out against the creation of Super Casinos, especially when this was seen as the only way to regenerate deprived areas (we should not be trying to solve social ills by preying on the poor and most vulnerable in our society), and I also spoke out against the war in Iraq (where we seemed to be going in without clear moral backing from the UN) to pick just two examples. I think that on both these occasions I was right to speak out – but then I would. The point is, if we feel concerned about something our politicians do or say, then we need to get across to them as best we can that we disagree. If we can do this in a polite and non-confrontational way, then that has to be for the best. Not every decision ever taken by a politician has been taken deliberately to annoy you or make your life harder – the chances are bad decisions have usually been taken in good faith.

There are so many big issues to tackle in our country, how can you choose to pack up your bags and barricade yourself in your bedrooms? As a Christian, the main drivers for me surround two key issues: Fairness and Equality.

In modern day politics, the words *'Fairness'* and *'Equality'* have become twisted to take on a new meaning. Whenever I hear a politician utter these words they tend to be either talking about the rights of women or the rights of homosexual people. (I am sure, statistically, in some cases they will be talking about the rights of homosexual women.) Whilst I have no truck with ensuring that women and homosexual people have equality of rights under law, under policy and in the wider political process, we need to ensure that we do not become side-tracked by ensuring our heart for justice in these matters also ignores fairness and equality for everyone else – regardless of gender or sexuality.

Positive discrimination is a great bugbear of mine. You do not tackle discrimination against one group by actively discriminating against another. Every action has a knock on effect. For example, why do you think that there has been such a rise in support for the BNP or UKIP or other parties on the far right of British politics? Is it coincidence, or are we perpetuating a system where white working class males feel they do not have a voice anymore?

If we really want to tackle the big issues of our time, we need to start by addressing wage inequality, unemployment (particularly youth unemployment), access to decent public services and the severe lack of homes and jobs outside the South East of England. We cannot solve these issues by sticking our heads in the sand, neither can we tackle them solely by a top-down approach – this needs to be something we are all invested in. We need to value people, pay them a Living Wage and ensure that the local hospital or school is as good and as reliable as those being run in the private sector. Fairness and Equality is about seeing the integral worth of our neighbours and ourselves – and seeing we all have a role to play in building a better, stronger nation where all can flourish.

So yes, we need better protection for gay people – but also for heterosexual people and bisexual people and transgender people where they face unfairness and discrimination. Yes we need better opportunities and representation for women at every level of business and politics – but we also need to ensure that people are judged on their merits and that, as a result, men are not shut out of these areas because of their gender.

What irritates me more than this is to be told what *'the big issue'* is for the next election. This is something I can decide for myself based on my own experiences and opinions.

"But banning fox hunting and putting a stop to the badger cull is 'the big issue' that will determine the next General Election." Really?

I am sorry, I love animals, and want to see them protected wherever possible, but I cannot get enthused about whether we allow a bunch of posh people to hunt foxes on horseback or instead allow these creatures* to be dispatched with a shotgun. Either way the animal is killed in a cruel and bloody way – all we are arguing over is how it should happen. That's the equivalent of arguing against sending people to the electric chair – but then instead of saying we should scrap capital punishment altogether, we say let's give them a lethal injection instead. (*In the interests of clarity, I am talking about the foxes rather than posh people here – I wasn't being deliberately ambiguous.)

A while ago, I was almost unfortunate enough to run over a badger. The badger is one of the longest, and slowest, of all God's little creatures.

Fortunately for the badger, he picked the one motorist whose car is actually slower than a badger at full amble.

I was driving a *'pacific green'* Skoda Felicia (I have no idea what the actual colour of the Pacific Ocean is, but I would be extremely concerned if it looked anything like the colour of this particular car), so even though the badger would have seen me coming, it wouldn't have escaped my wheels if I was a normal motorist coming down the road, due to its previously unparalleled slowness.

I am actually quite a conservative driver. I like reliability, I like fuel efficiency, I like safety, I like obeying the speed limit. Actually, it's the only area of my life where anyone can call me a natural conservative!

I feel I may now qualify to put up one of those annoying signs in my car window saying something like *"I slow down for badgers"*, but it is not going to change how I decide to vote.

Such discussions remind me of the great Pete Postlethwaite's speech in the equally great film *Brassed Off*:

"Over the last ten years, this bloody government has systematically destroyed an entire industry. OUR industry. And not just our industry – our communities, our homes, our lives. All in the name of 'progress'. And for a few lousy bob. I'll tell you something else you might not know, as well. A fortnight ago, this band's pit were closed – another thousand men lost their jobs. And that's not all they lost. Most of them lost the will to win a while ago. A few of them even lost the will to fight. But when it comes to losing the will to live, to breathe, the point is – if this lot were seals or whales, you'd all be up in bloody arms. But they're not, are they, no, no they're not. They're just ordinary common-or-garden honest, decent human beings. And not one of them with an ounce of bloody hope left. Oh aye, they can knock out a bloody good tune. But what the f*** does that matter?...And now I'm going to take my boys out onto the town. Thank you."

When we start ignoring the suffering of human beings, especially those at the bottom of society, the most vulnerable, those we think don't matter, or those that should work harder, or moan less, or get less support – and pretend what really matters is how we dispatch a fox, or whether we kill badgers or allow them to inadvertently kill sheep, cows and pigs through spreading disease – then we have real problems. Do I care about whales being hunted off the coast of Japan? Yes. Do I care more about people living in destitution, unable to heat their houses or put food on the table? Yes, I am afraid I do. And if you tell me *'the big issue'* at the next election is the implementation of the fox hunting ban, I am likely to give you short shrift, sorry.

But that's why we need an open discussion, a dialogue where we can all put our points forward, allowing them to be discussed in the public square and then – in the words of Brian Clough – decide that I was right all along.

What I am talking about is genuine engagement with the political process. I despair at the amount of *'networking'* within British politics.

I am sure we have all been told the importance of networking to our professional lives, but here and now I would like to start a one man campaign against aggressive, passionless, opportunistic networking that would make someone working in telesales blush.

The concept of networking is present at every level of politics. From the now not smoke-filled rooms in the Town Hall to the Champagne Receptions at Party Conference, it's the same principle wherever you go.

In fact maybe *'principle'* is entirely the wrong word. The one thing most networkers do not have is principles or self-respect.

The way networking works is that you find the most important person in the room and then you talk at them (start by telling them how big a fan of theirs you are, then tell them all about how wonderful you are, then finish by giving them your business card – that always works wonders) for as long as is necessary.

The problem of this is twofold. Firstly, the vast majority of people present are not going to be the most important person in the room –

therefore you will be repeatedly cutting people short and looking for a way out of being in their company. They may (not unreasonably) think you are a bit of a twonk. Secondly, the people you are targeting with your spiel realise they are important. This could go one of two ways – they might admire your brass neck and think *"Yeah, I'll give that bloke I met 5 minutes ago, who seems desperately enthusiastic about my contribution to the public discourse, a job"* or they might realise you are a serial networker only out for what you can get and they will cut you dead in order to go for a less demanding conversation.

Party Conferences are weird enough at the best of times. Part Party pep rally, where everyone comes together to pretend they get on, whilst politicians attempt to combine deeply moving political oratory with half-arsed jokes in an attempt to get 10 seconds on the national news that evening. You live off a diet of vol au vents and cheap wine, staying up till 4am in the vastly overpriced hotels in the hope of some tasty political gossip – you need to *'be seen'* and justify the fact you've paid over £100 on a ticket to sit in the balcony section for a whole week, when actually all you wanted was to be there for the one hour when the leader does his speech. The Conference is probably in a seaside town like Brighton or Bournemouth but due to the hotels being booked up months in advance you are staying in a small town no-one has heard of which is over an hour away from the actual venue. Trust me, these politicians are not going to be at their most sparkling and approachable.

The best and most effective type of networking is based around shared interests and genuine bonding. It's called relationship building – talking to other human beings you like about things you have in common. Networking is like going on a speed dating evening and opening the conversation by saying: *"I like you, you're great, will you marry me?"* It's unlikely to be seen as sincere and you are going to be looked upon with a great deal of suspicion.

Networking dictates that you only talk to people who are important – democracy is the opposite to this. Democracy is about listening to the views of everyone and finding a way forward. If I was going to get all spiritual on you here, I would say that the Gospel tradition goes even further – we should not be simply talking to people we deem to be important, we should recognise that everyone is equally important in God's eyes and that we have a moral duty to give a voice to the voiceless and those that society ignores.

See that's told you.

I have been very fortunate to get to know a lot of politicians personally. Not one of these relationships has been started over a glass of champagne at Party Conference. Predominantly I have got to know them through playing sport.

Throughout my time in Parliament I played football for the Parliamentary Football Team. This started, as all great sporting adventures do, when the team which was meant to be made up of MPs and Lords was running short of players for a particularly cold and rainy Tuesday morning game and they were desperate for anyone to come and make up the numbers.

Having been roped into playing, I played very well and the team decided that it would be rather good to keep me around in case they were ever short again. Over that 10 year period I played in nearly every single game that they had. Normally it would be against a small charity or organisation down at Burton Court in Chelsea on a Tuesday, but occasionally it would be playing at Stamford Bridge, Upton Park, The Stadium of Light, or even Wembley.

I can hardly believe that working in politics has allowed me such opportunities. There can be few professional players who have played at both the old Wembley and the new Wembley. It's a real honour.

Partly that experience was through being in the right place at the right time, but part of it was based on my own ability (I used to play football to a fairly high level, so I was always going to look fairly capable in amongst a team of what we could politely term part-time *'veterans'*) – the same is true of anything in life, you have to get out there and make your own luck. But you need to be yourself. Focus on what you are good at and you will soon find that not only will your contribution be welcomed, but you will soon be indispensable.

Sadly, my talents for catching a football and writing humorous throwaway political quips are unlikely to change the world – but I have every confidence that, with your mix of talents and unique outlook, you could achieve far more if you put your mind to it.

Don't give up on politics. The political process takes many different shapes and forms – and you have as much right as anyone else to influence it. Believe. Hope. Dream. Get involved. Never give up.

I'd like to finish this book with a short anecdote which hopefully illustrates the point I am trying to make:

An MP is talking to his young son trying to teach him simple mathematics. He shows his son a picture of 10 monkeys and 6 bananas. He asks how many monkeys won't get a banana. The son looks at his father, puzzled, and says that all the monkeys will get a banana. The frustrated father repeats his question: 10 monkeys, 6 bananas – how many monkeys will not get a banana? Again the son says that they will all get some banana. The dad asks one last time: *"How many monkeys will go hungry?"* The son replies: *"None will go hungry daddy. They can share."*

Sometimes we need to teach our politicians to look at the questions they face in a totally new way. There are no wrong answers, just different perspectives.

About the Author –

Kerron Cross was born on 21st August 1977 in High Wycombe, but was raised just outside Watford, to a Manx Mum and a Lancastrian Dad. A published writer in many fields and genres – his first book *"Drama, Verse, Sketches 2"* was published in 2001, published by CPAS Publishing and co-authored with Steve Tilley. His second book "A Dark Stranger's Guide To The Isle of Man" was published in June 2014 via Amazon. As a professional speechwriter, he has written articles for most of the UK national newspapers (both tabloid and broadsheet), as well as written for and appeared on TV, radio and online platforms. He worked for 10 years in the Houses of Parliament for two very nice MPs, spent some time working in Manchester for a Government Minister and then spent 4 years working for an Archbishop! He has also stood for Parliament in the 2005 General Election in the socialist stronghold of South West Hertfordshire and has 8 years' experience as a councillor on a local authority. He supports Watford FC (for his sins), Wigan RL and Lancashire CC. He is married to a Glaswegian (but not for much longer) and has a daughter called Blythe.

Printed in Great Britain
by Amazon.co.uk, Ltd.,
Marston Gate.